Tackle

Motorcycle Sport

This Way

ANTHONY DAVIS

STANLEY PAUL
London

STANLEY PAUL & CO LTD
178–202 Great Portland Street, London W1

AN IMPRINT OF THE HUTCHINSON GROUP

London Melbourne Sydney
Auckland Johannesburg Cape Town
and agencies throughout the world

First published 1963
This edition (revised) 1971

This book has been set in Times type, printed in Great Britain
on antique wove paper by Anchor Press, and
bound by Wm. Brendon, both of Tiptree, Essex

ISBN 0 09 103520 1 (cased)
0 09 103521 x (paper)

Tackle Motorcycle Sport
This Way

Contents

Illustrations

Foreword

I would like to dedicate this book to the memory of Bob McIntyre, for many years the greatest of private entrant road racers. He was kind enough, not long before his fatal crash, to contribute a foreword to the first edition.

I will not publish it now; instead I would like to say that in Bob were exemplified all the qualities to be emulated by sporting motorcyclists: skill in preparing machines, artistry on the track, courageous stubbornness that would never admit defeat even when matched against riders on superior machines, a cultivated physical fitness, unfailing sportsmanship and modesty and a perpetual readiness to help younger riders.

I am grateful to Bob for the time he spent talking to me about motorcycle racing. My thanks are also due to the Council of the Auto-Cycle Union for permission to quote from their General Competition Rules and other publications, to Suzuki (G.B.) Ltd., Lambretta Concessionaires Ltd., and the makers of A.J.S., B.S.A., Dot, Greeves, Seeley, Triumph and Velocette motorcycles for providing certain photographs.

Perhaps I should also acknowledge a debt to the Army who, years ago, let me make some of my earliest motorcycling mistakes on their machines. . . .

ANTHONY DAVIS

I

Introduction

THE sound arrives first, a snarling roar, and then the motorcycles flash past the pits, their goggled, helmeted, leather-clad riders flat long the tanks behind wind-cheating fairings.

Gears snick as the flying machines approach a bend, the bikes heel like yachts in a wind and then they are accelerating away again, out of sight, as gloved fingers open throttles and the tarmac streams beneath their tyres.

This is *road racing*, each man against the rest, most elemental and highly publicized form of motorcycle sport. But there are many others. . . .

Bikes buck over rutted tracks, the riders racing through clouds of dust to be first into a funnel of trees. They leap their howling machines into the air across a ditch like charging, mechanized cavalry.

This is *scrambling* or moto-cross, cross-country racing and the other great branch of the sport in which riders race against one another. In other competitions battle is against the clock.

The scene may be a seaside front. A rider on a machine with an outsized rear wheel covered by a treadless tyre hurtles from a startline as though fired from a gun, to cover a quarter-mile course in less than a quarter of a minute. This is *sprinting*.

There are also straightforward tests of riding skill. Competitors in cloth caps and berets stand poised on the footrests of their machines guiding them slowly up rocky gullies, through marshy morasses and down loose-surfaced slopes between tree-stumps, trying to keep their mud-coated machines moving without having to resort to using their feet. This is *trials riding*.

There are also grass and sand races, hill climbs, rallies and treasure hunts, concours d'elegance, motorcycle football and gymkhanas, and from time to time there are innovations like 'slalom' racing between straw bales on a quarter-mile course with midget 50 c.c. machines. All tastes are catered for in motorcycle sport.

There is something for every kind of rider. Girls as well as men take part regularly in trials, rallies, scrambles and even road racing. There is something for owners of all types of machine from beefy 750 c.c. Norton racers to diminutive scooters.

And there is something for every level of skill. At the top the great international events like the Isle of Man T.T. races and the International Six Days Trial in which professional or semi-professional riders straddle machines prepared regardless of cost and tuned by wizards in the business. At the other end the little trials organized by small town clubs for their own members only in which novices may compete on their workaday transport.

One can spend a fortune—or compete for virtually only the cost of petrol. It is open to everyone to decide for himself how far he wishes to go in the sport.

How the sport began

Motorcycle sport is practically as old as the motorcycle. At the turn of the century pioneer motorcyclists on machines with lozenge-shaped tanks, pushbike saddles, acetylene lamps—and pedals to assist the engines—were taking part in reliability trials —little more than long-distance tours but a sufficient test of those primitive machines, top-heavy, underpowered and erratic of steering. Soon cycling clubs were forming motorcycle sections and there were trials run at specified average speeds, sprints on the fronts of seaside towns and races on cycle tracks. Riders wore long leather coats, caps turned back to front and spare inner tubes and transmission belts around the shoulders.

In 1902 the Cyclists' Touring Club formed a motorcycle

section, then came the Motor Cycling Club. And in 1903 the Automobile Club of Great Britain and Ireland (now the Royal Automobile Club) formed the Auto-Cycle Club (now the Auto-Cycle Union) to register sporting motorcyclists, issue competition licences and adjudicate on records.

International racing followed, the first important race being held in France in 1905. On the Continent motorcycle racing was soon growing in popularity. In Britain it was handicapped, for here it was forbidden on public roads (as it is still), which was how the T.T. races, the world's premier motorcycling event, came to be staged by the Auto-Cycle Club for the first time in 1907 in the Isle of Man. For the island has its own Government and was prepared to close roads for racing. The same year the world's first real racing circuit was opened at Brooklands and the sport began to grow fast in Britain.

By the outbreak of the First World War races, hill climbs, sprints, trials and rallies were being held every weekend—as they are still today—except that today there are more opportunities for all to join in. On any weekend between spring and autumn no one is more than a few miles from a motorcycle meeting of some sort.

In the following pages I will introduce in more detail the various forms of the sport (omitting the professionally promoted spectacle of speedway), explain how to take part in them and offer hints on attaining success based on the example of great riders.

2

How to Start

THE first step for anyone who wishes to take part in motorcycle sport is to join a club. Virtually all competitions require membership of a club affiliated to the Auto-Cycle Union as a condition of entry.

At this point it will be as well to explain how the sport is organized and governed.

International control is in the hands of the Federation Internationale Motocycliste, or F.I.M., which has its headquarters in Geneva. Under the F.I.M. the Auto-Cycle Union controls motorcycle competitions throughout Britain and the Commonwealth, except for Canada and Northern Ireland.

All worthwhile competitions held in Britain are run under permits from the A.C.U., who license courses, check machines and equipment, approve timekeepers and generally see that the sport is properly conducted. The A.C.U. Competitions Committee has a dozen standing sub-committees, one dealing with moto-cross and others with road racing, the T.T. races, the International Six Days Trial and so on.

To finance its work the A.C.U. charges fees for issuing permits for sporting meetings and, where money is taken from the public, appropriates 3 per cent of the takings of the meeting in admission charges, parking fees and sales of programmes.

By the way, members of A.C.U. clubs are forbidden to take part in unauthorized motorcycle competitions; this is because such events, often staged by the social clubs of big firms, by local operatic societies and political groups, do not always observe the strict safety precautions insisted on by the A.C.U. and may in other ways do great harm to the sport. There have been, for instance, innumerable complaints in recent years from members of the public about badly organized rallies which roar through the same peaceful country towns and villages weekend after weekend, something the A.C.U. do not permit. At the time of writing, indeed, it seems likely that the Government will ban from public roads motor and motorcycle rallies which do not come under the control of the R.A.C. or A.C.U.

You may wonder who chooses the often-criticized but well-intentioned bosses of the sport. The F.I.M. is a democratically elected body of representatives from each of the member countries. For the record they are Algeria, Argentina, Austria, Belgium, Bulgaria, Canada, Chile, Cuba, Czechoslovakia, Denmark, Egypt, Finland, France, East and West Germany, Greece, Great Britain (also representing Commonwealth countries which are not members in their own right), Guatemala, Hungary, Indonesia, Ireland, Italy, Japan, Luxembourg, Mexico, Monaco, Mongolia, Morocco, the Netherlands, Nicaragua, Norway, Paraguay, Peru, Poland, Portugal, Rumania, Russia, San Marino, South Africa, Spain, Sweden, Switzerland, Uruguay, U.S.A., Venezuela and Yugoslavia.

Similarly, the A.C.U. is governed by a General Council comprising representatives from its national clubs (Scotland, Australia, British Guiana, Ceylon, East Africa, Malaya, Malta, New Zealand, Rhodesia, Singapore and Zambia); from its non-territorial clubs and from A.C.U. 'local centres' covering the whole of England and Wales.

In turn, each local centre is run by delegates from the individual clubs making up the centre. Which brings us back to the clubs.

Local centres and clubs

Clubs fall into two categories, the non-territorial and the local. The score of non-territorial clubs, affiliated directly to the A.C.U., are specialized organizations such as the National Sprint Associ-

ation, the Vintage Motorcycle Club, the Norton, Triumph and
Ariel Owners' Clubs, the Army Motor Cycling Association, the
British Motorcycle Racing Club, the Motorcycling Club of
Wales and the British Two-Stroke Club. But the body of the
organization is the local clubs. There are some 650 of them and
most big towns have one. In England and Wales they are attached
to twenty local centres which are as follows:

Cheshire (covering Cheshire, Flint, Denbigh, Caernarvon,
    Merioneth, Montgomery and Anglesey)
Cornwall
East Midland (Derby, Nottingham, Lincoln, Leicester and
    Rutland)
East South Wales (Radnor, Brecknock, Monmouth and eastern
    Glamorgan)
East Yorkshire (Yorkshire, east of a line from Yarm–Northaller-
    ton–York via eastern boundary–Goole)
Eastern (Norfolk, Suffolk and Essex)
Isle of Man
Midland (Shropshire, Staffordshire, Warwickshire, Worcester-
    shire, except for the southern part, and parts of Flint and
    North Gloucestershire)
Mid-Wales (Merioneth south of a line from Maentwrog to the
    junction of the Denbigh–Montgomery boundaries, Mont-
    gomery and Radnor, Cardigan and Brecknock, north of a line
    from Aberystwyth to Builth)
North-Eastern (Northumberland and Durham)
Northern (Cumberland, Westmorland and Furness area of
    Lancashire)
North-Western (Lancashire except for the Furness area)
South Midland (Northampton, Huntingdon, Cambridge, Bed-
    ford, Oxford, Buckingham, Hertford, Middlesex and parts of
    Berkshire and London)
South-Eastern (Kent, Surrey and Sussex)
Southern (Berkshire, Hampshire, Dorset and southern Wiltshire)
South-Western (Devon and southern Somerset)

Sporting machine—mini size. The Suzuki A.S. 50 Sports has a single-cylinder 49 c.c. engine

Sports machine—maxi size. The Triumph Trident has a three-cylinder 741 c.c. engine

Scrambling—A typical scrambles scene as riders descend a sharp incline. One climbs back to his machine after coming off

Road racing—Starting technique. After running three or four paces the riders drop their clutch levers and leap aboard side-saddle

Wessex (southern Gloucester, northern Somerset and Wiltshire)
West South Wales (Pembroke, Carmarthen, Brecknock and western Glamorgan, west and south of a line from Aberystwyth to Porthcawl via Builth and Aberdare)
Western (southern Worcester and northern Gloucester)
Yorkshire (all Yorkshire except that in the East Yorkshire centre)

Scotland, as I have said, has its own national club, the Scottish A.C.U.

Choosing a club

Normally one will join the club nearest one's home, but it is worth giving the choice some thought if one is keen to take part in a particular branch of the sport such as scrambling. Some clubs are more social than sporting; others, only a few miles away, may specialize in scrambles or trials. Your local motorcycle dealer will probably be able to tell you.

There are big clubs like Birmingham (motto 'Forward') which has more than 300 members. Birmingham Club has been in existence since the beginning of the century; famous members have included Freddy Watson, designer of the Watsonian Sidecar, and Rem Fowler, winner of the twin-cylinder class in the first T.T. in 1907. Today Birmingham boasts Jeff Smith, Malcolm Davis, Dave Langston and woman star Olga Kevelos. The club runs such major events as the British Experts Trial, and has fine clubrooms which are open for social events every night of the week.

There are also small clubs like Aberaman in South Wales with a membership of under twenty, which was formed in 1946 by half a dozen enthusiasts with £5 capital. Despite its smallness it was the first club in Wales to get permission to use a park for racing. It also organized the first road race to be televized 'live'. That was at Aberdare in 1955.

But whatever the size of the club, there one will find kindred spirits, help and advice. Scrambles, trials and racing riders, expert mechanics and tuners visit clubs to talk to members and

B

there are showings of instructional films. Many clubs stage stunt-riding demonstrations at local gymkhanas and carnivals and do much to improve the public's view of motorcyclists by 'adopting' a local charity. Invariably there are club outings and rallies, dances and other social events.

A number of centres publish gazettes giving news of forthcoming sporting events and also offering bargains in motorcycles, parts and accessories. Apart from the necessity of belonging to a club if one wishes to compete it is good to have the comradeship of other enthusiasts and ready access to knowledgeable and experienced motorcyclists. For this reason it is worth contacting a club, even if one has not yet acquired a motorcycle; members will be keen to guide the newcomer's choice.

I have not space to give a list of all the clubs here but the A.C.U. (address: 31 Belgrave Square, London, S.W.1) will be pleased to supply the addresses of those in any particular area of England and Wales or, for a shilling, send their official pocket handbook which gives a long list of clubs and secretaries' addresses and important fixtures during the year. For the addresses of Scottish clubs write to the Scottish A.C.U., 23 Torpichen Street, Bathgate, West Lothian. Addresses of organizations in other English-speaking countries within the F.I.M. jurisdiction will be found at the back of this book.

In passing it is worth noting that the R.A.C. allow motorcycle members of A.C.U. affiliated clubs to become associate members of the R.A.C. with the benefits of the get-you-home service, free legal advice, touring facilities, roadside telephone boxes and other R.A.C. services at a reduced subscription of £2 10s. instead of the usual £3 3s.

3

Machines

A BASIC essential for motorcycle sport is, of course, a motor-cycle. Nowadays there are specialized machines for each of the main branches of the sport, for each has different requirements. It will be appreciated readily, I think, that the ideal road-racing machine, designed for high speed on a tarmac circuit, is not ideal for trialling, which needs a machine that will pull steadily at low speeds over muddy, hilly terrain and rocks. Equally, a trials machine is not ideal for the cut-and-thrust hustle of scrambling or the explosive get-aways of a quarter-mile sprint course.

We will look at the special requirements of each branch of the sport and how it is met in the machines available in succeeding chapters. It is impossible to go far in the sport without specialized machinery, either bought as such or built by the rider.

These machines can be costly, an out-and-out racer costing over £600. (In fact they were relatively more expensive until 1962, when the Government removed purchase tax from racing machines, which had the effect of cutting their prices by some £90. This concession has not, however, been applied to scramblers and trials bikes.)

These specialized machines are usually transported to the circuit or venue in vans or trailers, such machines as road racers and scramblers in racing trim being in any event not only unsuitable for use on public roads but failing to comply with the requirements of the law.

How does all this affect the rider who cannot afford this kind of expense, who wants to use one machine for everyday transport and sport?

Fortunately it would be only rather expensive folly for the newcomer to sport to start with a highly specialized machine. He is well recommended to begin in standard-machine sport. Apart from rallies, at club and centre level there are also trials and even road races in which production machines, no more than mildly modified, are specified or will, at any rate, suffice.

It is time enough to think of buying or building a special when one has acquired some experience of the various branches of the game and discovered which appeals most—assuming that one wishes even to graduate to higher levels. Many of the greatest names in motorcycling began competing on standard machines. Bob McIntyre began his road racing on a 350 c.c. B.S.A. Gold Star which he borrowed from a fellow clubman. 'I removed the headlamp and silencer and that was my preparation done,' he told me. Yet he beat more suitable machines and won three of the events at his first meeting.

Equally many have switched their allegiance from one form of sport to another. John Surtees essayed grass-track racing and scrambling (just once!) before turning to road racing and becoming World Champion. Sammy Miller was a very good road racer before becoming our greatest trials rider.

Anyone with sporting inclinations (such as is presupposed by the reading of this book) would be wise to limit himself to a standard sports machine for his first ventures into competitive riding. Touring machines are built with an eye to comfort and economy on the highway; sports machines are designed more for good performance, strength and a fair ground-clearance.

Sports machines

Machines with sporting performances can be obtained in all engine sizes. Let us examine two of vastly different proportions to illustrate the diversity of machines and prices and the sort of performance offered.

Among the outstanding mini-machines is the 49 c.c. *Suzuki*

A.S. 50 *Sports*, a product of the Japanese firm which has been so successful in lightweight racing. It has disc valve induction and a five-speed gearbox.

Its single-cylinder, two-stroke engine of 41 mm bore and 37·8 mm stroke gives 4·9 brake horse-power at 8,500 revolutions per minute and its top speed approaches 60 m.p.h. It will give a commendable fuel consumption of around 109 miles per gallon at 40 m.p.h.

Other statistics:

> Compression ratio: 6·7 to 1
> Gear ratios: 10, 12·1, 15, 20·4, 35·7
> Tyres: 2·25 × 17
> Wheelbase: 46 in.
> Seat height: 29 in.
> Weight: 147 lb.
> Fuel capacity: 1·25 gal.
> Price: about £105

At the other end of the scale is the mighty *Triumph Trident*, with a three-cylinder 741 c.c. engine of 63 mm bore and 70 mm stroke giving 58 b.h.p. at 7,250 r.p.m. Big and heavy and not a machine for the novice rider, it is capable of passing 100 m.p.h. in third gear and, with three carburettors pouring on the power, flashing on to about 115 m.p.h. Overall fuel consumption is around 40 m.p.g.

Other statistics:

> Compression ratio: 9·5 to 1
> Gear ratios: 4·89, 5·83, 8·3, 11·95
> Tyres: front, 3·25 × 19; rear, 4·10 × 19
> Wheelbase: 56·25 in.
> Seat height: 32 in.
> Weight: 470 lb.
> Fuel capacity: 4·25 gal.
> Price: about £615

Incidentally, prices given in this book are generally those recommended by the makers. But prices charged now vary from dealer to dealer and by shopping around it is possible to find machines being sold for as much as £50 below list prices.

Subject to some general rules there is normally no restriction on the make, design or type of machine that may be used in a competition.

As I said at the beginning there are events even for scooters—a growing number of them—to which I will devote a later chapter. I will also deal later with sidecar sport, a field in which novices are unlikely to begin. (To me, the choice of a sidecar combination in preference to a solo machine is rather like choosing to fly bombers in preference to fighters. Yet many people do.)

Classes

The following classification of solo machines is followed. They are first divided into two categories A1 (Motorcycles) and A2 (Scooters), then each category is divided into classes according to the engine capacity, the divisions of the motorcycle category being as follows:

Class	Minimum engine capacity in c.c.	Maximum engine capacity in c.c.
50	—	50
75	50	75
100	75	100
125	100	125
175	125	175
250	175	250
350	250	350
500	350	500
750	500	750
1000	750	1000

To ensure that machines have not been bored out to give bigger capacity than the classes for which they are entered it is a general rule that every motorcycle finishing in a competition must, if required, be submitted for an examination and any motorcycle may be retained by the promoters for the time reasonably necessary for examination. Where it may be necessary for promoters to verify any fact this will be done at the cost of the rider, except that if measured to determine a protest the party against whom the decision is made must bear the costs. If the engine is found oversize the machine may be kept by the promoters until costs are paid.

Regulations

A number of riders like to build their own machines, known as 'specials' or 'bitzas'—from the old gag 'bitza this and bitza that'. They do it because they cannot find a ready-made machine which meets their requirements, or because they cannot afford such a machine, or just because they enjoy the challenge. They will take a Triumph engine, mount it in a Norton frame, add other features from an A.J.S., picking up these parts from machines broken up by garages. I know of a nineteen-year-old Manchester apprentice mechanic who finished in three National Rallies on a 500 c.c. twin he built by putting a 1938 Triumph engine in a 1955 Royal Enfield frame; the job cost him three hours a night for five weeks.

Other hybrid machines put up remarkable performances in sprint events. One must, however, be able to enjoy time spent in the workshop as much as time spent on the road, and a high degree of engineering aptitude is demanded.

Regulations relating to machines in competitions are of particular concern to builders of specials and those modifying standard machines and some of the most important may be noted here.

Solo machines must be equipped with an efficient brake on each wheel, operating independently.

Except in road racing and scrambling both road wheels must be protected by either a normal mudguard or by bodywork or streamlining giving the same protection. A 'normal' mudguard is defined as one which projects laterally beyond the tyre by at least ·4 in. (10 mm) on each side and covers at least 100 degrees of the circumference of a front wheel and 120 degrees of a rear wheel.

At the same time, the angle contained by a line drawn from the rear end of a mudguard to the centre of its road wheel and a line drawn horizontally through the centre of its road wheel must not be greater than 20 degrees.

In all races and sporting trials handlebar, clutch and brake levers must be of a type that end in a ball of three-quarters of an inch minimum diameter and this ball must be an integral part of the lever or a permanent fixture. (These levers can be bought for about 19s.)

In scrambles, grass-track races, hill climbs and sprinting self-closing throttle controls must be fitted, but they are not required in trials, competitions on the public highway, sand and road races.

Footrests must not be fixed more than two inches above a line joining the centres of the two road wheels. Metal studs, spikes, chains, rope or other non-skid attachments to tyres are prohibited. In most events machines must run on a commercial brand of petrol that can be bought at a filling station.

Without special A.C.U. permission, one must not carry any advertisement or trade sign on a machine in a competition other than the usual maker's or agent's transfer—so riders must not paint the fuel tank with an advertisement for their business!

The Clerk of the Course at a meeting has a duty to exclude any motorcycle the construction or condition of which he considers dangerous.

Choosing a machine

The learner is restricted by law to a machine of 250 c.c. or under as far as road riding is concerned, and for the inexperienced rider a 250 c.c. machine is big enough. The 250s are lighter and cheaper, yet have plenty of performance; they are not boys' bikes by any reckoning and are adequate for all forms of sport. I would not recommend a bigger machine to the inexperienced rider unless he intends to tour long distances. Nor would I recommend a motorcycle smaller than 200 c.c.; if one is sportingly inclined, one is liable soon to become dissatisfied.

When I began motorcycling the 350 c.c. machine was the most popular in the range. This is no longer so. Popularity moved to the smaller and the bigger—the 250s and 650s, and the trend continues. But the 650s are not for beginners.

It is important to choose a motorcycle of the right dimensions. A dealer put it: 'There are big 250s and little 250s. Some 250s are scaled-down 350s and some are scaled-up "tiddlers". You don't want one that needs a ladder to mount, nor one you can step over.' There are machines in the 250 c.c. class which are popular with beginners but which are comparatively small and a six-footer would not be comfortable on one. A rider of 5 ft. 5 in. or under might feel equally uncomfortable on another popular machine which is large for its engine size.

A rider should, in fact, be able to reach the controls easily while sitting in a relaxed position. If one is intending to service the machine oneself—and the country is not over-endowed with good motorcycle repairers—check carefully on ease of access to the working parts of the machine. And remember, when considering the price you can afford, to allow for any extras or accessories you may consider desirable.

When buying from a dealer go to one with a good reputation. With sport in mind, one who rides or has ridden competitively himself is preferable. Many do or did. A sportsman dealer and his staff will take an interest in your ambitions and give you valuable advice at no extra cost.

Buying a secondhand

Most people will prefer to buy a new machine, to be the first owner and be reasonably sure of trouble-free riding for some time. This is not always possible. When buying a secondhand machine, particularly from a private person, who does not expect to do business with you again, the old rule *'Caveat emptor'* (let the buyer beware) is a good one to bear in mind. If you are not knowledgeable mechanically take along someone who is to inspect the bike.

Look at the speedometer on the machine but never accept what it says unreservedly. The wear on handlebar grips and footrests sometimes tells a different story.

A clean machine—clean around the engine as well as the polished fuel tank—is generally (though not always) a cared-for machine. A muddy, battered machine may be in first-class condition mechanically but lack of attention to cleanliness suggests a similar lack of attention to maintenance. An oily engine may mean the bike is an oil-slinger to be avoided.

Bent footrests indicate a fall and may be a warning of a bent frame. Examine the tyres not only for the degree of wear, indicating how long it will be before new tyres are needed, but for uneven wear indicating something wrong with tyres, frame or wheel mounting.

With the machine on its stand grasp the rear wheel and try to rock it laterally; too much play may mean new bearings are needed. Spin the wheel to see if it runs true.

Pluck the chain over the rear-wheel sprocket. If it lifts easily from the sprocket it is a sign of wear; at the same time look at the sprocket teeth for missing or worn teeth.

Turn to the front end. Test the front-wheel bearings, forks and steering head by slackening the damper, if fitted, taking the machine off the stand, straddling it and turning the handlebars smartly each way from lock to lock, noting any clicking or roughness, then applying the front brake and rocking the machine.

Test compression with the engine warm. One should be able to balance one's weight briefly on the kick-start; if it sinks under one immediately there is compression leak. Start the engine and listen. Noisiness in itself is not very worrying, provided the noise is crisp and healthy, but if it sounds wrong something probably is wrong. Suspect blue smoke emitted every time the throttle is opened. Slow pick-up suggests a dirty carburettor.

Check the gear-change for smooth, positive feel, and if possible try the machine on a longish road test.

Don't be too eager to snap up a machine even if you are told others are after it. You may lose a bargain; you may well be rid of an old banger. Try a counter offer to the price asked; it is customary these days to ask a price several pounds above the figure for which the owner is prepared to settle.

Money matters

There are four main ways of paying for a motorcycle. *Cash down* is the simplest and cheapest if you can manage it. If you cannot, *hire purchase* is the easiest way of obtaining the machine. At the time of writing one is expected to put down a one-third deposit and pay off the balance over two years. But hire purchase is expensive; the machine does not belong to one until the final instalment is paid (by which time pride of ownership has certainly gone and the bike may be a wreck), while in the event of the buyer's death the hire finance company may take back the machine, unless relatives choose to continue payments under a revised agreement.

It is cheaper and better to finance the deal through a bank, by which means the machine becomes one's property from the start. It is also, unfortunately, harder. There are two methods. One is to obtain a *personal loan*.

Better still is an *overdraft*, but one needs to be on good terms with a bank manager to get one these days. There is no fixed rate on interest for overdrafts; it varies according to the amount required, the time for which it is required and the security one may be able to offer, but a major advantage is that interest charges are calculated only on the outstanding amount after each payment, not on the whole period of the overdraft.

4

Clothing

WHAT about personal kit? First comes the helmet. Over the past decade more and more riders have taken to wearing helmets and today the great majority do so. In the past the Minister of Transport has considered making them compulsory, with fines of up to £50 for lidless riders. While no one welcomes the idea of compulsion, their adoption has certainly cut the number of fatalities appreciably.

Helmets are worn in virtually all forms of motorcycle sport except trialling, in which the headgear is commonly a beret, stocking hat, ski-cap or cap, which traditionally is as disreputable as possible. (Scott Ellis has been widely conceded to hold the honour of appearing in the scruffiest of the lot!) But there is a move towards the adoption of helmets for trials.

In competitions and practices for them, where speed is a determining factor, A.C.U. regulations require the wearing of a helmet of a design approved by the A.C.U., and the Clerk of the Course or his deputy is empowered to impound any helmet considered to be of incorrect pattern or to have become ineffective (the same stipulation may be made in the supplementary regulations for other competitions).

The A.C.U. standard is a particularly demanding British Standard specification, and A.C.U. approval is denoted by an endorsement on the neck-curtain.

There are over fifty varieties of helmet on the market ranging in weight between 1 lb. 3 oz. to 2 lb. 6 oz. and in price from

£3 to £20. All consist basically of a rigid shell of wood pulp or glass fibre containing a cork lining to absorb shock.

Main differences in style concern the fitting of a peak (sometimes detachable) and the shape—where the choice is between the orthodox and the 'bone dome' space helmet of fairly recent introduction. These are matters of individual preference. Peaks are good when riding into bright sunshine and in heavy rain, and are popular in scrambling, but are not favoured for high speed. 'Bone domes' offer greater protection around the ears, but impair hearing to some extent.

It is of paramount importance that a helmet should fit properly. The forehead should be put in first and the helmet should sit squarely and levelly. A too tight helmet will cause considerable discomfort. It is better that the helmet should be a trifle loose as one may expect to get hot. But if a finger can be inserted inside the helmet at the temple it is too loose. Do not try to pad such a helmet. If you have a really odd-shaped head a helmet may be moulded on a hatter's last at little or no extra cost.

Slack in a chinstrap may be taken up by a folded handkerchief which will also serve the function of protecting the jaw from the vibration of the petrol tank in road racing. (Despite the pad fitted to road-racing machines for this purpose, riders have told me that they are unable to shave for days after the T.T. week because of the soreness of their chins.)

Helmets should be cared for scrupulously. They should never be hung up by the chinstrap as this stretches the harness. When wet they should be allowed to dry gradually, away from heat. Despite care, the mixture of normal wear and tear, sweat and hair-oil will weaken the harness in time, and it is recommended that it should be renewed, or the helmet replaced, after about eighteen months.

After a crash in which the helmet has suffered it should always be replaced; consider that if it has saved your life it has earned its cost.

Many riders paint a badge or personal emblem on their helmets. This is not pure vanity; apart from lending a personal touch and making one's helmet easy to sort out from a pile in a clubroom, it enables a signaller to identify one swiftly in a race or scramble.

Goggles

With the helmet go goggles. Eyes are precious and sensitive. Apart from the danger of being hit by a flying stone or getting a piece of grit or an insect in an eye at speed, the lashing of the wind can cause inflammation. Goggles must be non-splinterable and, although it is more expensive, laminated glass is preferable to cheap plastic lenses which tend to scratch and discolour.

Curved lenses give better vision than flat ones. To check for optical distortion hold the goggles at arm's length, look through them at a telegraph pole or lamp-standard and rotate them through different planes.

R.A.F.-pattern goggles costing about £1 5s. are probably the most popular. They give distortion-free vision in all directions and replacement lenses are available.

Tinted eyepieces are available which are valuable in bright sunshine but should not be worn in poor visibility or at night, as they inevitably cause some loss of definition. It is also possible to buy special goggles for wearing over spectacles (which should also be unsplinterable), or, at a cost of about £6, to buy goggles incorporating prescription lenses.

Headbands are made of either fabric or rubber. Fabric bands stretch, which is a good point if the goggles have to be lifted over a helmet-peak, but they are inclined to slacken in rain and shrink on drying. Rubber stretches less.

To avoid permanent stretching, goggles should not be left around the helmet after use, and they should never be folded across the nose-piece.

To avoid draughts which will affect the eyes at speed the goggles should fit well. Badly fitting ones can be sealed by sticking on pieces of foam plastic with Bostik.

Goggles should be cleaned daily before use. There are various anti-mist compounds on the market or in an emergency soft soap, a cut potato or plain spit will serve. John Surtees is an advocate of the spit method. I have sat with him and watched him carefully polishing his goggles before a race; apart from its practical value I think it gave him something to occupy himself with during the tense moments of waiting.

As an alternative to goggles, swivelling visors can be bought for about £1 10s. They are acceptable for town riding and can be raised or lowered easily, but are prone to shift under high wind-pressure and I would not recommend them for use in sporting events.

Leathers

Now as to the body. . . . For road racing or racing on similar hard surfaces regulations require clothing to be of leather. The leathers worn by the professional riders are tailored for them from horse-hide, generally padded as protection against tumbles and cost £25 to £40. As with most things, the expensive ones last longer than the cheap ones.

For other competitions there is a wider choice, except that in all speed competitions the regulations require a 'jacket or long-sleeved jersey or other garment of material of at least equivalent strength to a serge battledress blouse'.

The qualities required, varying in degree according to the type of competition, are, of course, some measure of protection in a fall, protection from the weather and freedom of movement. Don't forget that one may have some footslogging to do.

Don't confuse showerproof and waterproof. Showerproof clothes will stand up to only a limited amount of rain.

The most popular clothing is the two-piece suit in p.v.c. plastic or proofed nylon. Long coats are out of favour today. Plastic is prone to tear; proofed nylon is exceedingly strong but much more expensive. Weights vary considerably. Suits costing less than £9 are probably not worth buying and the cost of better ones runs up to about £17.

A towel around the neck will prevent rain finding its way inside the clothing; it is also a good idea in wet weather to wear the trousers *over* the boots, but trouser legs should not flap or they may snare the kick-starter or footrests.

Some riders I know advocate a swimsuit beneath the clothes to absorb perspiration in scrambles, others favour the lightest underwear. But a body-belt of canvas or leather is a sensible precaution in scrambles, where the stomach muscles take a good shaking and, if one falls, one runs the risk of having a tyre manufacturer's name inprinted round one's middle by the front tyre of a pursuing rider. The cost: about £2 10s.

Gloves, which cost from about 35s. to £5, are compulsory in speed events and desirable generally. On a rally machine with extensive handlebar shielding a light pair will be sufficient. On other models heavier gauntlets, which wrap round the sleeve, are preferable. But gloves should not be so heavy as to make the feel insensitive, nor so big that a fold forms across the palm. Trials riders sometimes use two pairs in bad weather—a thin pair for use when riding the tricky 'observed sections' and a heavier pair to cover them while riding the road sections in between.

Boots

Good protection around the feet and legs is essential for all riders; most knocks are about the legs and ankles.

In speed events long leather boots (without studs), or boots with strong leg-attachments, are compulsory, except for sidecar passengers who, as acrobats, are permitted to wear plimsolls.

Again, competitors in other branches of the sport have more choice and trials riders often favour short rubber Wellingtons costing about £2, with thick football stockings underneath to pad them.

Leather boots are probably the best because leather breathes, the only snag being that they are difficult to waterproof. Plentiful applications of dubbin are recommended or there are liquid silicone treatments.

Boots may be pull-on or lace-up pattern but should fit well and must allow sensitive operation of brake- and gear-levers and

Sprinting—Ian Ashwell with his 998 c.c. Vincent Satan, about to clock 158 m.p.h. at Brighton

Trials machine—The 250 c.c. Greeves 24 TE 'Scottish Trials'. Note the short, high exhaust and the bulb horn

Trials riding—Martin Lampkin balances on the footrests as he takes his 128 c.c. Alta-Suzuki through Welsh mud

Trials riding—Eric Adcock negotiates a typical trial rock section. Note how he picks out a flat rock and approaches it straight on

should allow one to run with a machine. Ex-army despatch-rider boots are popular.

Professional riders may wear out three pairs of boots a year, for boots take heavy punishment. In cornering they often scrape the road, while hooking up the gear-pedal wears out the toecap of the right boot, and swings on the starter damage the arch. (A cobbler can fix protective patches.)

Since boots cost £7 to £8 they deserve care. Never dry wet boots before a fire, it can cause them to crack. Stuff them with balls of newspaper and let them dry out in their own time in an airy place.

5

Entering

ONE may begin taking part in competitions twenty-one days after being accepted as a member of a club.

Competitions—by which are meant trials, races, record attempts and other sporting events beyond the merely social ones —fall into five main groups:

Closed to Club, which are limited to members of the organizing club.

Centre Restricted, which are limited to members of clubs belonging to the same local centre.

Regional Restricted, open to riders from more than one centre but not all.

National, open to riders from all parts of the country.

International, open to riders of more than one nation.

For the first three of these classes (in which the entry may be further limited by the division of events into classes for riders of different degrees of experience) membership of a club is sufficient qualification. For national events a licence (£1 a year to club members) is needed from the A.C.U. or Scottish A.C.U., while before one is eligible to compete in international events one must have qualified in national events. Reasonably enough, no one can begin a racing career in, say, the T.T. races; he must first prove his worth in lesser events.

Supplementary Regulations

Forthcoming competitions are announced in centre journals and the motorcycling papers. From the secretary of the meeting one then obtains the Supplementary Regulations and an entry form.

Supplementary Regulations give details and rules of the particular competition, telling the competitor all he needs to know. Properly drawn up they are set out like an army battle order under five headings.

The first is the *Announcement*. It includes the name of the competition and the promoter, the date and venue, the type and number of the permit under which it is held and the persons and types of vehicle eligible to compete.

Under the second heading, *Awards*, comes the list of prizes, the method of allotting them and conditions attaching to them, such as the period for which they will be held if not to be won outright. If no awards are being offered—an unlikely event—this will be stated.

Under the third heading, *Entries*, come the date and time by which entries must be received, the address to which they must be sent, the amount of the entry fee and insurance premium, if required, conditions as to the minimum and maximum number of entries that will be accepted, how they will be selected if too many apply (which happens frequently), and conditions regarding the return of entry fees.

Under the fourth heading, *Officials*, will be listed the stewards of the meeting, the timekeeper, judge, handicapper, machine examiner, clerk of the course and the secretary of the meeting with his address.

The information given under the fifth heading, *Description*, includes the time and place of the start, the length and nature of the course, details of practice periods and rules concerning identification numbers, outside assistance and protests.

Other information varies, according to the nature of the competition.

In the case of *speed events* it includes the rules regarding protective clothing and helmets, brakes, footrests, streamlining, mudguards, exhaust pipes, removal of parts such as registration plates and the specification of fuel to be used.

It gives the direction of racing, how the course will be marked, the method and order of starting, the maximum number of starters in heats and finals, details about refuelling and flag signals and rules regarding leaving the course, finishing, timing and handicapping.

In the case of *trials* and similar events the information will cover the rules regarding tyres, compliance with legal requirements, the starting order and intervals between starting, route marking, whether route cards will be issued and, if so, when and where, details of observed and non-stop sections and how they will be indicated, rules about bulking, restarting within a section after 'failure', missing a section, artificial boundaries, definitions of 'footing', 'failure' and crossing an artificial boundary. (All these terms will be explained later.)

Where the event involves time, speed and special tests the regulations will give the scheduled speed, time checks, method of control, time allowances including any allowance for late starting and delays, timing arrangements and a description of special tests such as braking, acceleration and stop-and-go tests, how performance will be assessed, details of penalties, bonus marks and the method of marking for special tests.

Entry forms

The entry form calls for the name, address, licence number or club of the rider (and his entrant in a race where the driver is not also the entrant), the make and category of motorcycle, the events to be entered, details of the entry fee enclosed and, in the case of speed events, the premiums for insurance.

It also incorporates an indemnity clause which reads like this:

'I have read the Supplementary Regulations issued for this meeting and agree to be bound by them and by the General Competition Rules of the Auto-Cycle Union. In consideration of the acceptance of this my entry I agree to save harmless and keep indemnified the —— Club, the —— Centre of the A.C.U. and the A.C.U. (including the owners or lessees of the land used for the

meeting) and their respective officials, servants, representatives
and agents from and against all actions, claims, costs, expenses
and demands in respect of death, injury, loss of, or damage to,
the person or property of myself or my passenger(s) or mech-
anic(s) (as the case may be) howsoever caused, arising out of, or
in connection with, my entry or my taking part in this meeting
and notwithstanding that the same may have been contributed to
or occasioned by the negligence of the said bodies, their officials,
servants, representatives or agents. I declare that I am not less
than sixteen years of age. I declare that whilst taking part in this
meeting I have an operative policy of insurance as required by
the Road Traffic Acts.' (The last sentence is omitted on entry
forms for speed events.)

In the case of entrants and drivers under the age of eighteen
the form has to be countersigned by a parent or guardian. Where
the entrant is someone other than the rider he also must sign.
There is no need to be frightened by the awesome legal phrases;
the form is a standard one.

Fill out the entry form carefully. Any entry containing a false
statement is void and the entry fee may be forfeited. Any entry
not accompanied by the entry fee is void.

Assumed names
I cannot, offhand, think of any good reason for competing under
an assumed name these days, but, as a matter of interest, the
A.C.U.'s rule number 138 says: 'A person shall not take part in
any competition under an assumed name unless special permission for the use of such assumed name has been granted by the
A.C.U. In such cases a licence will be issued in the assumed
name, if approved, on payment of an additional fee.' (It costs
£1.) The rule goes on: 'The licensee, for so long as he is registered
under an assumed name, shall not take part in any competition
under any other name and shall not revert to the use of his own
name until he has obtained a fresh licence in his own name from
the A.C.U.'

An assumed name has to be indicated on any official programme between inverted commas, which seems rather to give
the game away.

Over-subscribed meetings

Entries for a national competition close at least fourteen days
before the date of the competition. For a restricted competition
entries may be accepted up to two days before the date and for a
closed competition up to an hour before the time of the start.

Entries with the appropriate fees (which range from about six
shillings for a centre trial to £3 for a T.T.) may be made by
telegram and telegraphic money order provided they are received
within the time limit, but such entries have to be confirmed by a
proper entry form sent off on the same day as the telegram.

It is well to get one's entry in early as many trials and races are
over-subscribed. If the number of entries exceeds the maximum
number laid down in the Supplementary Regulations those to be
accepted will be chosen usually in order of their receipt on a first-
come, first-accepted basis or by ballot, unless one is a crowd-
drawing star.

Promoters are entitled to refuse any entry provided they notify
the entrant in writing as soon as possible (within 48 hours after
the closing of entries at the latest in the case of national competitions).

Entrants should hear of the position with regard to their entry
—whether it has been accepted, held in abeyance or refused—
within seven days of putting in the completed entry form. Riders
whose entries have been held in abeyance or who have been
offered reserve positions are entitled to enter another event on
that day provided they notify the first promoter in writing of the
withdrawal of their original entry. It is against the rules to fail to
ride in a competition for which one has entered and ride in another competition at another meeting on the same day.

It is also against the rules—and bad manners too—not to turn
up for a competition for which one has been accepted. Someone
else may have been robbed of a chance to compete.

Normally a change of rider or passenger, or the make or capacity of a motorcycle, may be considered by the Secretary of the Meeting after entries have closed, provided the entrant notifies him in writing at least 24 hours before the official starting time of the competition of some 'good and sufficient reason' why the entered rider, passenger or motorcycle is unable to take part. It is not usually permitted to make any such changes after the start of a competition.

In the case of international, national and restricted competitions the promoter has to send a copy of the detailed provisional results to every entrant within fourteen days.

Insurance

How does one stand in the event of an accident while taking part in motorcycle sport?

The rider's normal insurance policy covering riding on the highway usually excludes 'racing, pace-making or speed testing'. It will generally cover trials riding and rallying, but it is essential to check this with one's insurance company before taking part in any sporting events.

Under an A.C.U. scheme the *promoter* of a meeting is automatically granted third-party insurance cover when they issue his permit, and the policy indemnifies the A.C.U., the centre, the club and officials in respect of their legal liability for injury to persons or damage to property following an accident. Insurance against accidents to officials is also covered at the same time.

Competitors in speed events have to be personally insured for at least the following benefits:

£500 in the event of death, the loss of two limbs, or two eyes or one limb and one eye.

£250 in respect of the loss of a limb or an eye.

£5 a week during temporary total disablement (limited to fifty-two weeks and excluding the first three days).

Medical expenses up to 15 per cent of an admitted temporary total disablement claim.

The premium, which the rider normally pays with his entry fee, is only a matter of a few shillings for sprints and hill climbs. Premiums are little higher for scrambles and grass track events. For all other races, international meetings and meetings lasting more than a day, premiums vary according to the nature of the course and the event. In a T.T. they run into pounds.

Trialling and social events are not covered by the scheme, though a club can insure all riders in trials for around a shilling a head.

Riders planning a busy season of racing are recommended to take out policies to cover the whole season of sport. The benefits would normally be additional to those paid by the national scheme, but one may contract out of the national scheme provided the A.C.U. approve the cover given by the policy. (It is in the rider's own interest that the A.C.U. experts should 'vet' it.) It may also be worth while to insure racing machines against damage during racing and in transit.

Details about insurance can be obtained from C. T. Bowring and Muir Beddall (Home) Ltd., of The Bowring Building, Tower Place, London, E.C.3, the official insurance brokers to the A.C.U. and R.A.C.

6

Rallies

IT IS not within the scope of this book to teach the rudiments of riding a motorcycle. To any reader who has not yet learned to ride let me recommend the Government-backed R.A.C.-A.C.U. Training Scheme, which provides motorcyclists and scooterists with the opportunity to undergo initial training on private ground before taking to the public roads.

The scheme, operated in many towns throughout Britain, consists of twenty-four tuition periods, both theoretical and practical, lasting nine to twelve weeks. Anyone over sixteen can enrol; training machines and insurance cover are provided. The cost to the learner is £1 16s. The course culminates in the R.A.C.-A.C.U. proficiency test, which demands quite a high standard of skill and knowledge.

Certainly I believe that one should be a competent rider before taking up competitive riding. One should have learned to balance a machine at slow speeds, to turn in the smallest possible circle without having to 'foot', to recognize treacherous road conditions and be able to deal with skids. (The well-known rule is to steer into a skid; that is to say, if the back wheel starts to slide to the right, steer to the right.)

Further experience can be gained in the social type of club events and in rallying, the cheapest and most light-hearted form of motorcycle sport. This is standard-machine sport in which roadgoing machines from scooters to speedsters are used in normal trim, and the cost is virtually no more than that of petrol.

Pillion passengers are often carried as navigators and aides or just for company. It is sport for all; one does not have to be a Mike Hailwood or Dave Bickers to get in the awards lists.

What rallying involves

Strictly speaking a rally is a competition where riders endeavour to travel over public roads from start to finishing point at a pre-set average speed, checking in at 'controls' on the way. Usually it ends with certain special tests and sometimes there is also a concours d'elegance, an 'extra' which does not affect the rally results. Marks are won and lost for timekeeping, the number of controls visited and for expertise in the special tests.

'Treasure Hunts', in which competitors are sent off to discover inn signs, numbers on letter-boxes and the like, may be good fun, but should not be confused with rallies, as often happens.

On the Continent rallies cover vast distances and several days, and there are big money-prizes, but here they are usually one-day or weekend affairs with small cups or plaques as the awards. There are, however, some big events in which there may be several starting points for the benefit of riders from different parts of the country.

One needs a reliable watch or stopwatch, a mileometer with an accurate trip in tenths and a useful accessory is a Blackwell Calculator, a plastic-disc device for working out average speeds.

Route cards and maps

In some rallies route cards are issued. They may give the names of places, distance from the last place and arrows to indicate changes of direction, or they may detail the route in a similar way to the route cards supplied for touring by the A.A. and R.A.C. with abbreviations such as S O for Straight On, L and R for Left and Right. But some rallies involve navigational problems. One is given the location of a number of controls to be visited, and skill is required in deciding the best route to cover all the controls and keep to the time schedule.

Sometimes a control will be designated by a six-figure map

reference on a one-inch Ordnance Survey map. (This is a map on which one inch equals a mile on the ground and showing great detail—woods, orchards, bridges, electricity grid lines, telephone boxes and even whether a church has a tower or a spire.)

The maps are divided into squares by vertical and horizontal lines. To find a six-figure reference such as 598182 on a given map-sheet, one first finds the vertical line bearing the first two figures—in this case 59—then the horizontal line bearing the fourth and fifth figures—in this case 18. Then mentally divide the square that is to the right of the vertical line and above the horizontal line into ten equally spaced vertical lines and the same number of horizontal lines. Look at the third figure of the reference—in this case 8—and count that number of imaginary vertical lines to the right. Look at the sixth figure of the reference—2 in my example—and count two imaginary lines up. Where the imaginary horizontal and vertical lines meet is the point one wants. This is a very accurate method of reference.

The job can be done more quickly with the aid of a device called a Romer. (Price: 7s.)

Where time allows one can make up one's own route cards with the aid of a map. The information needed is a matter of personal opinion but common practice is to have six columns with the information set out like this:

Total miles covered	Place (with controls in capitals)	Road number	Miles to next control	Time due	Total miles to go

Route card-holders may be bought or made from plywood and Perspex with clips for attaching to the handlebars. They should of course be waterproof. In rallies where map-reading on the road is involved and particular sheets are not specified, map-books will be found easier to handle than a large map-sheet which flaps in the wind—but there is always the irritating moment when one runs off one map-page on to another.

The premier British rally is the National which ends in a different town every year and gets an entry of some 750 riders. (It has been more than 1,000 in the past.) One can cover 600 miles in the 24-hour event, riding at a scheduled 25 m.p.h. Riders plot their own routes to take in controls spread over the country, and there is a host of awards not only for class winners but also for the best performances by riders from different clubs and centres. Too easy? I have known more than 200 fail to finish.

Preparation

Rallies are particularly popular with the one-make clubs and scooterists, and there are also events for owners of pre-1931 vintage machines. William Martin, a Berwick-upon-Tweed bank manager, rallied a 1903 Ormonde machine with belt-drive transmission, stirrup-type cycle brakes and no springs, which he bought for £5 and rebuilt.

As machines take part in rallies in normal touring trim little preparation is essential, though care will, as always, be repaid. In events involving night riding particular attention should be paid to the lighting system, the more so since rallies are usually held in summer when lights may have been little used for some time. Extra lamps may be useful for spotting signposts and turnings swiftly, but do not overtax the charging system. A powerful torch will have innumerable uses.

Make sure tyres are fit for the journey ahead and ensure that handlebars, saddle and footrests are adjusted to give a comfortable riding postiion. A prop stand is desirable to save hauling a heavy model on to a centre stand.

A full tool-kit should be carried. Its contents are a matter of individual choice, but I suggest puncture outfit, tyre levers, sparking plug, nuts and bolts, spare bulbs, valve cores, spanners, pliers and screwdriver, chain spares and rivet-extractor, tyre pump and pressure gauge, insulating tape, rubber bands from an old tube, electric cable and copper wire. (John Surtees insists, 'Never go without a length of copper wire; it's got so many uses.')

A pannier is almost essential for housing food, toilet articles, sweater, spare goggles and machine-cleaning materials.

As rallies are run mainly on the highway, insurance must be in order and the driving licence should be both current and signed.

Special tests

Apart from rallies, special tests are also used as tie-breakers in many trials. Typical is the braking test. The rider sits astride his machine with the engine dead and in neutral gear, behind a line A. He faces down a hill. At a signal he pushes off with one foot and allows his machine to coast down the gradient. He must stop with the front wheel on or below a line B, perhaps 70 yards on.

The rider's time is clocked from the start signal to the moment the front wheel crosses line B. Also measured is the distance beyond line B of his front wheel when he stops. Time and distance must both be as short as possible; the winner is the man whose combination of time and stopping distance are shortest.

The difficulty is that by slowing to stop exactly on the line one increases the time figure; by sailing over the line before halting one cuts the time but puts up the distance figure. The system of marking should be studied—it varies with different organizers—to see whether one evil is preferable to the other.

There are acceleration tests in which one starts and rides to a point, usually uphill, the art being in deciding which gear to use to achieve the fastest time. Sometimes acceleration and braking tests are combined, while another popular test is a freewheel 'slalom' between posts.

The key to success in special tests is a calculating, unflustered approach.

Preparing for a concours

I suppose a concours d'elegance can be likened to a beauty contest for bikes. But a concours is not necessarily won by the newest machine or the one carrying the biggest quantity of chrome or badges. Whitewall tyres, and all the accessories of a Halford's branch, are not essential to win. The judges, though their systems of marking may vary—sometimes incomprehensibly—look more for evidence of care lavished on the model.

A concours usually takes place on the day following a rally, which means road dirt has to be removed before the machine can be brought to its best.

Wash down with soapy water, or use a mild detergent. If the bike is really caked with mud a rag soaked in paraffin may be used. While there is nothing to beat a good wax polish, unless one wants to spend all night working on the model, employ a combination cleaner and polish which can be applied and removed swiftly.

This is an occasion for 'bull'. Do not forget to clean *underneath* the crankcase and in other places often overlooked; judges have as keen an eye for spotting dirt as an inspecting R.S.M. in the Army.

7

Trials

SOONER or later rallying and standard-machine sport will fail to satisfy the keen rider and the best starting point in more serious, specialized motorcycle sport is trials riding.

Normal half-day or one-day sporting trials involve a ride of from 15 to 70 miles, competitors starting at one-minute or half-minute intervals. But the parts that count are the 'observed sections'. These may be close together or separated by miles of open road. They may include sheep tracks deep in oozing slime or baked in hard ruts, marshland, woodland, steep rocky gorges and steps, flooded lanes and water-splashes.

The aim is to ride these sections with the loss of the minimum number of marks, the marks being customarily deducted like this:

For *dabbing*, a quick prod at the ground with one foot to maintain balance: 1 mark.

For *footing*, which is paddling along with the feet, or anything more than dabbing: 3 marks.

For *stopping*, which includes falling off the machine: 5 marks.

The observers' cards are checked at the end of the day and lost marks totalled, ties sometimes being decided by special tests such as those described in the section on rallying.

Some observed sections are comparatively easy to ride feet up, others are impossible and footslogging is inevitable, though hardened 'mud-pluggers' frequently moan that modern trials are too easy. All clubs have favourite sections within easy distance.

Speed does not enter into sporting trials (except that a time may be set within which the course must be completed), for a trial is a test of riding skill in the face of natural hazards and not a race.

Why do I call trialling a good starting point for the novice? Because it is relatively inexpensive; an everyday machine may be modified to suffice, although obviously it cannot compare with a specially built trials model. Because engine size means less than in any other branch of the sport. Because there are so many trials at all levels of the game and they are held all year round (though they are fewer in the summer months when keen 'mud-pluggers' consider the weather too good to make cross-country hazards interesting, despite the artfulness of organizers who create artificial handicaps by narrowing paths and creating bends with tapes). Because advancing age is little handicap. And because trialling develops mastery of a machine in a way which must help towards success in other branches of the sport.

Many road racers and scramblers ride in trials during winter to keep their hands in although, among the experts, trials riding is now as specialized as other branches of motorcycle sport. It has its measure of trade support and there are works teams but, even so, most of the stars are only part-time riders. Gordon Blakeway is a Darlington market gardener, Scott Ellis a Longbridge car-factory worker and sidecar expert Peter Wraith a research engineer in Cheshire.

At club level, trials riding is still an amateur sport, at which the novice can be sure of a welcome. There is no barrier against girls in trialling. Some, like Mary Driver, now Competitions Manager of the A.C.U., and Olga Kevelos of Birmingham, have had considerable success.

Trials machines

The trials machine, since it will have to run on public roads between one observed section and the next, must comply with all legal requirements such has having speedometer and horn and displaying its road-fund licence.

Scooter—The Lambretta Grand Prix model

Scrambler—The 380 c.c. Greeves Griffon

Scrambling—Watch out for ruts. Arthur Lampkin (250 B.S.A.) has his wheels in a well-worn one as he races for the finish at Shrubland Park

Scrambling—One takes off when topping a rise at speed. John Banks (498 c.c. B.S.A. Victor) demonstrates mastery of machine while airborne

The ideal machine is light, compact and narrow, whatever its engine capacity. It must pull steadily at walking pace and yet respond readily to a tweak of the throttle. Wide ratio gears are employed, a very low first gear for the tough sections and a highish top gear for use on the highway.

The engine has lowish compression and a heavier-than-usual flywheel, and manual ignition to aid even slow running; a light-alloy cylinder head and cylinder barrel to save weight.

The machine will have a short wheelbase and good ground-clearance—at least 7 or 8 inches. There will be few projecting parts, and vulnerable parts of the engine may be protected by a steel-plate shield.

The fuel tank is small, to save weight and to enable a good steering lock to be provided. (Where necessary the lock may be increased on a standard machine by filling down the steering stops and imposing dents in the fuel tank by placing a metal bar against it and clouting it with a mallet.) Handlebar grips should be of non-slip type; they cost only a few shillings to buy.

Mudguards are narrow and at least two inches from the tyres to avoid mud clogging between them and the tyres, though some makers and riders like to set the lower end of the mudguards nearer the tyre than the front end to stop too much mud entering. The front mudguard must not be too short at the fore-end or the rider will be pelted with mud.

The front wheel will be narrow but of large diameter, the rear wheel will be strongly spoked and capable of taking a wide tyre, usually of four-inch section.

Since tyres will be run at low pressures security bolts—one in front, two at the rear—are essential to hold the tyres to the rims. Suspension in the front will be on the soft side, to absorb the shock of hitting rocks.

The saddle, which may advantageously be of rubber so that water will not be absorbed when the machine is hosed down, will be high enough to allow the rider to rise easily on the footrests. The footrests will be broad and strong since the rider will frequently be standing on them. They will be as short as practicable

D

and 10 to 12 inches from the ground to avoid obstacles. For the same reason the footrests may also be slightly upturned and backswept, the kick-start will fold and the exhaust system be up-swept, and no centre stand will be fitted.

A good air cleaner is essential since the machine will be ridden through clouds of sand, chalk and dust. Carburettor, magneto, H.T. leads and plug covers will be waterproofed. (A section of car-tyre inner tube makes a good waterproof sleeve for the carburettor.)

Specials can be built for trials riding and standard machines modified on the lines to meet the requirements I have indicated, but it is difficult to match the ready-made trials machines. Unlike the situation in road racing, similar mounts to those used by factory teams are available to all.

Two popular mounts

The trend in trials and scrambles machines in recent years has been to providing them in kit form. This has the great advantage of avoiding punitive purchase tax, so anyone capable of assembling a motorcycle from the parts and drawings supplied can save a fair amount of money.

Let us take a look at two trials bikes which are sold in this form.

The *Cotton* 170 *Trials* is a bike which has competed without disgrace against the dominant Spanish machines from Bultaco and Montesa. It has a Minarelli die-cast alloy engine of 60 mm bore and stroke.

There is a wide range of rear sprockets available to provide different gear ratios for different types of terrain. The 65-tooth sprocket gives ratios of 14·1, 18·5, 22·4 and 35, while a 52-tooth sprocket gives 11·4, 14·8, 17·7 and 27·5. Other sprockets available are 50, 58, 60 and 70 tooth.

Other statistics:

> Compression ratio: 8·5 to 1
> Tyres: front, 2·75 × 21; rear 4·00 × 18
> Wheelbase: 51 in.

> Ground clearance: 10·5 in.
> Weight: 185 lb.
> Fuel capacity: 2 gal.
> Price: £210 in kit form

Cheaper still is the revolutionary *Gaunt-Jawa*, produced and ridden to good effect by Peter Gaunt at the end of 1969. True, its Jawa engine is only 89 c.c. but it is not a toy. The two-stroke, single-cylinder rotary-valved power plant develops 11 b.h.p. at 5,600 r.p.m. on a 25 to 1 petroil mixture. And it has a five-speed gearbox with bottom gear of 49 to 1.

Other statistics:

> Compression ratio: 8·5 to 1
> Tyres: front, 2·75 × 21; rear, 4·00 × 18
> Wheelbase: 50·5 in.
> Ground clearance: 11·5 in.
> Weight: 150 lb.
> Fuel capacity: 1·1 gal.
> Price: £175 in kit form

It should be noted that while trials machines comply with legal requirements, they are sold in trials trim, which may not include lighting. Equipping such a bike with direct lighting to enable it to be ridden on the road at night costs about £7. The chief problem to decide is what size of machine to buy. There are good machines from 125 c.c. to 500 c.c., but British makers have been more successful with lightweights than the bigger machines, and the bigger the machine the higher are running costs and depreciation.

Unless of heavyweight build, the novice would be well advised to begin with a 200 c.c. or 250 c.c. model.

Riding

Trials riding can be learned only by practice and experience. First, however, watch some trials in which top riders are competing. The greatest is undisputedly Belfast-born Sammy Miller, 5 ft. 10 in. tall and 10½ stone in weight, many times winner of the A.C.U. Stars on his 497 c.c. Ariel, and still the best on the Bultaco 250 c.c. machine which he has used in recent years.

Then get an experienced rider to go into the country with you (making sure not to trespass) and practise. The first lesson to master is learning to ride standing on the footrests. Most observed sections need to be ridden this way, except where weight is needed on the rear wheel. The body should be poised, balanced. 'Body lean', the art of swaying the machine past obstructions, has also to be acquired. Learn to pull back on the handlebars to help the front wheel over a rock step.

Find a typical trials section, preferably one used by a local club, and practise until it can be ridden 'clean'. Techniques must vary according to the rider and the terrain.

Typical hazards

Mud and rocks are the two biggest hazards. Where mud is shallow and the ground is flat it can be ridden slowly and cautiously in bottom gear. Where it is deep and sticky, or the ground is uphill, one needs a higher speed to get through; the deeper the mud or the steeper the hill the greater the speed required. Bends should be taken in as upright a position as possible to avoid losing balance.

With practice one will become expert at classifying the mud and picking the shallowest path through it, and some sections will be ridden in second gear. The danger of this is that if one makes a mistake and has to change down it costs momentum and sometimes balance. One must also be on guard against wheelspin from too much acceleration.

Marshy ground generally needs some speed to avoid bogging down, but with too much speed steering control becomes impossible.

Rocky ground has to be taken slowly so that one can pick a path between the bigger boulders. Unavoidable rocks should be hit squarely. More speed is needed over smaller stones, but one has to watch for them shifting beneath the wheels and robbing one of balance.

Watery hazards are met by maintaining fairly high engine revs and slipping the clutch to keep water from the exhaust pipe, proceeding slowly so as not to cause a bow wave, and being prepared for potholes or boulders beneath the water.

Downhill stretches can be more taxing than uphill ones. Normally one lets the machine run, using the exhaust-lifter if fitted, and dabbing at the front brake, but on acute descents one must slow to the lowest possible speed, using the exhaust-lifter and both brakes and slipping the clutch if necessary; the rear wheel must not be allowed to lock.

The use of feet must be related to the penalty-marking system; if, as occasionally happens, the penalties in a trial are the same for dabbing as for footing, then if one has to put out a foot one may as well get full marks' worth, have a good 'foot' and make sure one has regained balance properly.

The first event

Before taking part in a trial insurance coverage must be checked. Most companies allow trials riding without extra payment; however, the company should be contacted. Remember also that while one may take part in events held on private ground, although disqualified from holding a driving licence, a trial may well pass along a section of highway, in which case a driving licence is necessary and the machine must be licensed and fit for the road.

Check the machine's waterproofing, adding rubber sleeves to electrical leads if necessary. Make sure the road-fund licence-holder is waterproof too, and see that the carburation is even. Adjust the saddle so that one can switch easily from sitting to standing position yet still be able to foot. One should be able to hold the bars comfortably while standing on the footrests with the knees slightly bent. If necessary, adjust clutch and brake levers so that they come readily to hand.

The tool-kit should include spare levers and a spare plug, while many riders tape duplicate cables to their machines, alongside the ones in use, in case of breakage.

On arrival at the venue the rider should report to the secretary and may be required to sign in. Clear up with the secretary any problems. Competition numbers will be issued, if not allotted earlier, and can be fixed to the machine where directed with rubber bands cut from an old inner tube. A route card may be issued, but often the route will be marked by cards bearing arrows, or by coloured cards or powder, blue signifying 'Turn Left', red for 'Turn Right' and white 'Straight On'.

Tyre pressures should now be lowered. To assist wheel-grip rear tyres will be worn at from three to nine pounds according to whether the going is mainly mud or rocks—or up to twelve pounds per square inch if there are long distances to be covered on the road. Front tyres are run a pound or two harder.

The event should begin sharply on time. Published times are supposed to be adhered to strictly in all branches of motorcycle sport, and though events may sometimes start late they must never, in any circumstances, start early.

Riders will be despatched at one-minute or half-minute intervals. On reaching the first section one will probably find a queue. Dismount, park the machine, inspect the hazard and decide how to tackle it, whether it can be rushed or needs taking slowly.

If in any doubt about what is required, check with the marshal in attendance, before starting. Don't worry or despair if you are very slow. Tommy Robb, the Honda road-racing star, recalls that when he rode in his first trial on a standard touring machine at the age of sixteen he lagged so badly the organizers sent out a search party to look for him. 'At least I took home a finisher's award,' he says.

After the trial is over

If the trial is held under wet conditions be prepared to find that your brakes have suffered loss of efficiency; apply them lightly while riding along until the heat has dried them out sufficiently to restore their bite.

After the event both rider and machine are likely to be hot, sticky and plastered with mud. It is sensible to take a change of clothes which a friend can look after, also washing materials for freshening up.

Try to hose down the machine, using detergent if necessary, before the mud is dry. Then rub over with an oily rag and run the engine to complete the drying-out process. If the dirt has dried or is persistent a paraffin-soaked rag is useful. If one is doing a lot of winter trialling it is a good idea to protect the machine by brushing on a 25 per cent mixture of petrol and engine oil. The petrol evaporates to leave a film of oil, which does not look beautiful but serves its purpose.

Awards

The rewards for success? Awards in a Centre Restricted trial are commonly of this pattern:

A Premier Award for the best individual performance.

A Novice Cup (a novice being a person who has never previously won an award—though some meetings do not count awards won in a Closed-to-Club events).

A Cup for the best performance on a 350 c.c. machine, or smaller. A Cup for the best performance on a machine of over 350 c.c. A Cup for the best girl rider.

First-class awards—small prizes or certificates—to the next best 10 per cent of competitors. Second-class awards to the next best 10 per cent. Third-class awards to the next best 10 per cent. (It depends on the size of the trial whether third-class awards are made.)

There are also usually awards to the best performers from each club in the centre.

Long-distance trials

Not to be confused with the short sporting trials are the rare long-distance events taking several days. They are very different. Some riders like to spend their holidays taking part in the Scottish Six Days Trial held every May in beautiful country around Fort William at the foot of Ben Nevis.

This combines the observed sections of a trial and the time-schedules of a rally. Altogether riders cover nearly 800 miles in the six days, taking in nearly 150 observed sections. They can also lose marks for being late at control points, in special tests and for faults in their machines.

Different again is the International Six Days Trial, held in different countries. (When it is Britain's turn the venue is a wild part of Wales or the Isle of Man.)

No marks are lost for footing in this; it is something of a cross between a scramble and a rally. Competitors ride about 300 miles a day on roads and paths, trying to maintain set speeds. Vital components are sealed for the duration of the contest and the machines are locked up overnight, little time being left for maintenance. Although private entrants take part, this is primarily a team event and is dominated by factory teams. It is a costly event to compete in and is for experienced trials riders only.

8

Scrambles

EXPERIENCE in trials is valuable in scrambling; one will have learned much about riding different kinds of terrain and many riders take part in both sports.

Scrambling is said to have been born at Camberley, Surrey, in 1924, when some club members planned a new kind of trial. It was to have no observed sections but was to be a straightforward race across country. The A.C.U., shocked, refused to allow such an event to be called a trial. The organizers discussed other names until one of them laughed and said, 'Whatever we call it, it'll be a rare old scramble!' And scrambling was born, though nowadays the Continental-favoured name, moto-cross, is equally commonly used. Scrambling is so popular today that several heats are often needed to whittle down the number of competitors in a race.

Television has helped to popularize scrambling in recent years; it is certainly a spectacular sport, rough and tough. Hawkstone Park, the country's most famous circuit, which is between Shrewsbury and Whitchurch, has had attendances of over 70,000. Hawkstone is a one-and-a-quarter-mile-long circuit with such self-explanatorily named features as Wood Roughs, Sand Pits, Hairpin and The Gully, apart from high-speed sections. It is also notorious for its dust, which envelops riders in dry weather.

Because average speeds over scrambles circuits are only of the order of 30 to 35 m.p.h. scrambling is a very even sport. Modest cash prizes are customary, so it is possible for a skilful rider to cover his main expenses.

There are two scrambles classes, 250 c.c. and 500 c.c. In both classes there are world championships and British championships, formerly known as A.C.U. stars.

Britons like Suffolk motorcycle dealer Dave Bickers on his Greeves, and Arthur Lampkin of Yorkshire and Jeff Smith of Lancashire on works B.S.A.s, have excelled in the smaller class, but there has been a lack of factory support in this country for the 500 c.c. class which allowed Swedish riders such as Rolf Tibblin and Bill Nilsson on Husqvarnas to achieve supremacy in the heavier category.

Tibblin, who worked 16 to 20 hours a week on his machines, practised for scrambling by riding in snow—something which British riders have fewer opportunities of doing, although I know Dave Bickers has enjoyed it.

Machines for scrambling

Lamps, front registration plates and licence holders must be removed for scrambling. Clutch and brake levers must be ball-ended for safety, the ball being at least $\frac{3}{4}$in. in diameter and either an integral part of the lever or a permanent fixture. Ends of footrests have to be rounded with a radius of at least $\frac{3}{8}$in. Throttles must be self-closing.

Mudguards must normally be worn, the rear one covering at least 35 degrees of the upper rear quadrant of the wheel, though permission may sometimes be given for the removal of the front mudguard. Exhaust pipes must not project beyond the machine.

These are official requirements, but what are the desirable features of a scrambler?

It needs punchy acceleration and the ability to pull hard all the way through the range from low revs (this applies particularly to the big machines).

It needs a first-class air-filter to trap dust and sand. Stands are not used and the kick-starter usually folds to avoid projections like tree-stumps and rocks. The gear-change lever is usually set high and so are the footrests—to avoid obstructions when cranking the machine over on a bend.

The saddle should be positioned so that one can rise on the footrests to a semi-standing position, while, when sitting comfortably, one's hands should rest on the (non-slip) grips with the arms slightly bent. Expert riders develop a trick of operating the brake lever with the forefinger only. Incidentally, clutch and brake levers should not project, or fingers can be trapped or the front brake applied violently if one clips an obstruction.

Knobbly competition tyres are essential and, to prevent creeping, security bolts (one on the front wheel, two on the rear) should be fitted as in trialling.

Tyre pressures are worn low, though higher than in trials. In the wet and in mud a rear tyre may be as low as four pounds per square inch, though on hard, dry ground the pressure may be as high as twelve pounds. The front tyre is usually inflated a couple of pounds heavier. Never run with too soft tyres in scrambles, or there is a risk of bursting a tyre on striking rocks at speed.

What the makers offer

As with trials machines, the majority of scramblers are now sold in kit form.

Although Britons can buy the Husqvarna 400, the world-champion machine in the 500 c.c. class, it costs £565 in kit form, which makes it the most expensive scrambler on the British market.

So let us look at the Greeves, the product of Britain's most famous makers of moto-cross machinery. The Essex firm's contender in the big class, which has been ridden with considerable success by Vic Allan, is the *Greeves Griffon* 380. Its 380 c.c. engine of 82 mm bore and 72 mm stroke develops 39 b.h.p.

Other statistics:

> Compression ratio: 10·7 to 1
> Tyres: front, 3·00×21; rear, 4·00×18

Ground clearance: 10 in.
Weight: 227 lb.
Fuel capacity: 1·5 gal.
Price: £395 in kit form

In the 250 c.c. class A.J.S. returned to scrambling in 1970 with the *Y4 Mark 2* which soon won a name for its good riding position and handling and the cheapness of spares. The 247 c.c. Stormer engine is a single-cylinder two-stroke of 68 mm bore and stroke.

Other statistics:

Compression ratio: 11 to 1
Tyres: front, 2·75 × 21; rear, 4·00 × 18
Ground clearance: 9 in.
Weight: 218 lb.
Fuel capacity: 2 gal.
Price: £375 in kit form.

Another recent entrant in the small class has been the *Suzuki TS 250 Savage*, which has a 246 c.c. single-cylinder two-stroke engine of 70 mm bore and 64 mm stroke developing 23 b.h.p. There is a five-speed gearbox.

Other statistics:

Compression ratio: 6·62 to 1
Tyres: front, 3·25 × 19; rear, 4·00 × 18
Weight: 280 lb.
Fuel capacity: 1·96 gal.
Price: £350 in kit form.

I would strongly recommend starting with a 250 c.c. machine; apart from being cheaper, there is a bigger selection in that field and it is a more popular class.

It should be noted that scramblers are usually sold, naturally enough, in scrambling trim—that is, without such impedimenta as registration plates, horn, speedometer, licence-holder and road-going silencer—and if it is intended to ride one on the highway they must be added to comply with the law. Allow about £10 for this.

Number plates

It is customary to require competition numbers to be painted and displayed on three plates. They must be solidly made, 9 inches by 11 inches and elliptical in shape, flat or slightly curved. One is carried facing forwards and not more than 25 degrees from the vertical and the others face outwards and are vertical, one on each side of the machine. The figures must be at least six inches high and three and a half inches wide, the strokes an inch thick and with an inch between figures.

Colours will be specified in Supplementary Regulations, but paint must be matt. A tip from veteran sidecar-racer Bill Boddice: to avoid an accumulation of paint on his plates by the end of a season he paints the numbers on with whitewall rubber-tyre paint, which is unaffected by rain but can be wiped off with a paraffin-soaked rag.

Practising

Get to the paddock early and walk round the course, noting stones, rocks, dangerous tree-stumps and the texture of the ground. Consider the overtaking and braking points, remembering that one may be baulked on the most obvious lines, which will also become gouged and rutted. Work out alternative lines. In dry conditions it is usually better to keep to the earth, avoiding any grass, for grass is always slippery; in wet weather the grass will probably be safer than the earth.

Sign in at the marshals' table and when practice begins—there must always be a practice—put in a few laps, watching for deepening ruts if the ground is soft. These may become tricky after racing has got under way.

Ride feet-up as far as possible. Dab if you must, but never use your feet as props; scrambling isn't speedway, and this is an easy way of spraining an ankle. Watch the experts at practice. You may learn something, though the top men contrive to give little away. Their crafty technique, which you can adopt when you are skilful enough to be watched by others, is to learn the course in sections, going fast on a different section each lap but never showing their hands by riding the whole circuit at their fastest speed.

Have an apple or a sandwich before the race. It is as bad to race on an empty stomach as a too full one. See that the engine is warm for the start by keeping it wrapped in sacking if necessary. When called to the line—scrambles are started with the riders in one long line abreast—keep the motor running until the signal to stop engines.

Starting

In scrambling a kick-start is normally used. (It would not be practicable to push-start machines as in road races, because of the rough nature of the ground.)

Operate the kick-starter to bring the engine on to compression. If possible find a hillock on which to put the left foot to make balancing the machine easier. Be ready for the starter's flag, or the release of the elasticized tape which is used at some circuits like Hawkstone. (Watch the starter's arm in the case of a flag, his foot if he is to press a tape-release pedal or the end of the tape if his foot is out of sight.)

As soon as flag or tape begins to move, swing down on the starter and follow through, hooking the gear-pedal up into first gear on the way back. (Some courses have downhill starts where second may be used, but I recommend making a routine of starting in first and changing up almost immediately.)

The noise of machines starting all around will be off-putting because one cannot hear or feel one's own engine. The only answer is confidence in oneself and one's machine. Feed in the clutch and get away.

In events having clutch-starts—that is, with the engine already running—have the engine revving at about half throttle and feed in the clutch as the starter moves, but don't release the lever too smartly or the front wheel will come off the ground in a bucking-bronco manner which is better suited to the opening of a Lone Ranger film than to the start of a motorcycle race.

A rider who 'jumps the gun', by moving forward too soon

while under starter's orders, is usually penalized by the addition of a minute to his final time. A rider who fails to reach the starting area in time to come under starter's orders is not allowed to join the race.

Riding

As in trialling, rocks and mud are the two major natural hazards. Rocks can buckle a wheel if hit at too fast a speed. But rain and its effects are a more frequent problem.

In deep mud the technique is to go as fast as possible, carrying out braking when in a straight line, for mud grips the front wheel like tramlines in a road. The same advice applies to deep sand (more common in Holland than here).

The rule for water-splashes is to go in slow, so as not to cause a bow wave, then accelerate out. Always brake earlier and make gear changes sooner in the wet.

To clear ditches look for a ramp up if possible and gun the bike off this launching pad. Acceleration is needed on take-off to lift the front wheel, so that the machine will land on the rear wheel first. Throttle back while in the air and open up again on touchdown. But remember the aim is not to fly the farthest, however good it may look on TV and in the motorcycling papers. One cannot steer in the air, and the bike is not being driven while it is aloft, so get down as soon as possible and get under power again.

A small reserve of power on downhill stretches can be valuable in allowing acceleration to avoid an obstruction.

Probably the greatest art in scrambling is throttle control; wheelspin should be kept to a minimum.

Tactics and signals

Tactics? In a long race it may be possible to play a waiting game, but in a short race, particularly on 250s, it is unquestionably best to try to get to the front from the start. Overtaking is not always easy on a scramble course. But, as a novice, don't ride over-hard. This leads to trouble. While little quarter is given in scrambling, deliberate baulking of faster men or barging of slower ones is frowned upon.

If you come off, but are able to continue, do not let any spectator touch your machine. 'Outside assistance', other than that of an official acting in the interests of safety, will bring exclusion.

In a long race a signaller may be needed to pass information. He should be someone on whom one can rely, and stationed where he can be spotted easily. The scrambles rider speeding over rough country cannot give attention to the blackboard signals used by road racers. A 'thumbs up' to indicate all is well, arms stretched wide apart to indicate a good lead, held close together to denote a narrow one, or a squeezing motion to indicate someone is trying to climb into your exhaust pipe—these are the sort of signals to arrange. The extension of two fingers can take on the meaning, 'Two laps to go'.

Flags

One may also receive signals from officials—flag signals. They are:

Red: All riders stop immediately.

Black (with a rider's number)*:* That rider stop.

Yellow (motionless)*:* Danger, go carefully.

Yellow (waved)*:* Great danger, be prepared to stop.

Green: Course clear.

Chequered black and white: Finish.

Only officials are allowed to use flags, which are supposed to be at least 2 ft. by 2 ft. 6 in.

The chequered flag is displayed as the winner crosses the finishing line and is then kept flying. Each rider is waved off as he crosses the line after the flag is displayed, and must not start a fresh lap. Positions are decided by the number of laps each have completed, those who have done the same number of laps having their positions determined by the order in which they finished.

In the case of a dead heat, the riders tying for a place share the prize for that placing. When two or more tie for a place the next rider to finish is placed according to the numerical order of

Road racer—350 c.c. A.J.S. 7R. For many years the mainstay of
Junior races all over the world

Road racer—The 500 c.c. Seeley. More modern but in the same
tradition

Road racing—How to take a corner. The riders lean into the bend as Alan Shepherd (Aermacchi) leads the way in a 250 c.c. race at Oulton Park

Road racing—This picture shows a starting grid as riders line up for a race at Silverstone. Front row usually goes to those who were fastest in practice

finishers—for example, if two men finish equal first, the next man home will rank as third.

Machine care

Scrambling is hard on clutches. Clean the plate tongues with a file and replace plates regularly. Because sand and dust penetrate everywhere the magneto and carburettor must be cleaned regularly, while the air cleaner should be washed in petrol.

Tyres should be checked after every meeting for cuts and cracks. Chain maintenance is also important; chains take considerable punishment, and a weakness can rob one of success in an infuriating manner.

E

9

Road Racing

ROAD racing is to most enthusiasts the ultimate in motorcycle sport. During the season from April to October the top riders form a travelling circus between the 'classic' races—the Grands Prix of Spain, France, Belgium, Italy, Ulster, East and West Germany, Finland, Czechoslovakia and the Dutch T.T.s and, of course, the greatest of all motorcycle events, the Isle of Man T.T.s. On these events depend world championships, decided by points earned for places in the major races.

Road racing is dangerous—as evidenced by the unfortunate number of fatalities in recent years. It is also costly—and the rewards, even for the stars in the classic races, are not as high as might be imagined.

International riders are today reduced virtually to three classes: those who are works-sponsored, those who have private incomes and those Commonwealth riders who tour the Continental meetings, living roughly in caravans.

There is another reason, apart from the paucity of prizes, why it is hard to get into the very top bracket. The ambitious rider cannot buy the type of expensive multi-cylinder machines which win world-championship events. It is not simply a question of money—though racers are the costliest machines in the catalogues. The unbeatable MV Agustas and Gileras of the 'fifties and the Hondas and Suzukis of the 'sixties have been available only to riders the factories have chosen to sponsor or support.

Once upon a time virtually all manufacturers included racers in their catalogues. Now the number of thoroughbreds has shrunk depressingly, particularly in the lightweight classes in which most development has taken place in recent years.

The backbone of racing was, in fact, made up for years, of just four models, the Norton 350 and 500, the A.J.S. 350 and Matchless 500.

These well-tried machines which constituted the majority of entries in races all over the world, and on which riders like Luton engineer Phil Read and Lancashire carpet fitter Alan Shepherd rode to the front, are still being raced extensively and there is a big second-hand trade in them.

The *A.J.S. 7R*, once known as the 'boys' racer', has a 349 c.c. single-cylinder engine of 75·5 mm bore and 78 mm stroke. It peaks at around 7,800 r.p.m.

Other statistics:

> Compression ratio: 12 to 1
> Tyres: front, 3·00 × 19; rear, 3·50 × 19
> Wheelbase: 55 in.
> Seat height: 27 in.
> Weight: 284 lb.
> Fuel capacity: 4·75 gal.
> Price when last made: £420

Catalogued racers

Direct descendants of the A.J.S. 7R and Matchless G 50 are the 350 and 500 c.c. machines produced in Kent by Colin Seeley, once a British sidecar champion. The *Seeley 350* engine has the same bore and stroke as the 7R's.

Statistics:

> Compression ratio: 12 to 1
> Tyres: front, 3·00 × 18; rear, 3·50 × 18
> Wheelbase: 55 in.
> Seat height: 28 in.
> Weight: 280 lb.
> Fuel capacity: 3 gal.
> Price: £628

The machine can, however, be fitted with a five- or six-speed Schafleitner gearbox instead of the standard four-gear one at a cost of around £75. Two gallon or four gallon tanks for short-circuit and grand prix events can be substituted for the standard tanks. Engines can be bought for £283 and there are also a variety of kits of parts.

In the bigger class of racing which has become increasingly popular, partly due to the Japanese dominance of the small class events, Seeley is concerned with the Gus Kuhn company in making a 750 c.c. short circuit racer based on the Norton Commando.

It uses the standard 745 c.c. twin-cylinder Commando engine but it is extensively modified for racing, with a rebalanced crank-shaft, balanced conrods, high compression 10·25 to 1 pistons, a racing camshaft and gas-flowed cylinder head. There is a five-speed Quaife gearbox and a Seeley frame. The cost: £850.

Bought separately, the frame kit costs £350, the gearbox £135, the engine, modified for racing, £240, alternative engine and rear wheel sprockets, £1 17s. 6d. each.

Don't think that competitive lightweights are likely to be greatly cheaper. The incomparable Yamaha 250 c.c. racers can be bought over the counter but cost £955 (which includes a £255 kit of spares). The Yamaha 350 costs £1,000, including £262 worth of spares.

Racing machines are, of course, thoroughbreds, designed for speed and produced inevitably in small numbers. That is why they are expensive.

To complete the outfit a fibre-glass streamlining shell is needed, costing £12 to £35. When streamlining was permitted in the Manx Grand Prix for the first time in 1962 it was calculated by those in the know that the shells clipped 15 seconds off times on the island's 37¾-mile circuit.

The usual form of streamlining today is the 'dolphin', seen in the illustrations of road racing. 'Full-frontal' streamlining, which was becoming more and more enveloping, was banned from racing some years ago, just in time to stop riders disappearing completely from the view of the spectators.

One also needs a variety of sprockets, because different circuits and weather conditions require different gearing, and a van or trailer to convey the racer to the circuit.

The professional, or semi-professional, road racer—the number of full-time British professionals can just about be counted on the fingers of your hands—find it necessary to have a number of machines. To make a reasonable income he needs to compete in at least two classes and have a couple of machines in each class. The privately entered rider often spends winter working on two of them, one in each class, modifying gearboxes, brakes and frames and fitting special pistons. These will be his first-choice machines the following summer. At the same time he takes delivery of two new machines which will serve as his reserves until the next winter, when he can work on them, and the cycle will commence all over again.

Clubman's racing

What I have written so far will sound depressing, but the picture is not as gloomy as it may appear, particularly for the rider who has no ambitions to become a world champion.

Secondhand racers can be picked up at half the cost of new ones. A glance at the columns of the motorcycling papers will disclose advertisements such as '1954–60 7Rs, £140 to £295', and 'Yamaha 250 road racer, one of the fastest in the country, £425'. Many will list the machine's history; its previous rider-owners and race successes.

For those with more workshop skill than money there is Bantam racing. Bantams are the little motorcycles ridden by Post Office telegram boys but there is little resemblance in racing trim. Although the machines must retain the basic 125 c.c. engine, standard crankcase and three-speed gearbox, some will reach 100 m.p.h. Yet a complete racer can be built up for less than £100. Secondhand Bantams are advertised for as little as £40 so this is easily the cheapest form of road racing available.

For those who want a bike that they can race and also use as a touring mount there are production races. Possibly due to the boring dominance of Japanese machinery in racing and the failure of British attempts to build bikes to beat them, production machine racing has grown enormously in recent years. And there are a number of clubman's races at circuits such as Brands Hatch and Snetterton in which production machines, carrying full touring equipment such as lights, horns and silencers must be used.

In some respects these races are the descendants of the first T.T.s, which were intended for fully equipped production touring machines, an intention which was backed in the first races by the rationing-out of petrol on the scale of 90 miles per gallon for singles and 75 miles per gallon for twins. T.T. stands, of course, for Tourist Trophy and the race came into being quite largely because British manufacturers objected to their Continental counterparts running specially built racing machines in the existing major races. Today's T.T. machines are a long way removed from that 'tourist' category.

Clubman's machines

Unquestionably the most popular machine in production races in recent years has been the *Triumph Bonneville T 120*. There is probably no production race in Britain which has not been won by a 'Bonny'. In the 1969 Isle of Man international production race Bonnevilles were first, third, fifth and sixth.

The Bonneville is a 649 c.c. twin of 71 mm bore and 82 mm stroke, with twin carbs and cams, developing 47 b.h.p. at 6,700 r.p.m. and has a speed of more than 116 m.p.h.

Statistics:

> Compression ratio: 9 to 1
> Gear ratios: 4·88, 6·04, 8·17, 11·81
> Tyres: front, 3·00 × 19; rear, 3·50 × 18
> Wheelbase: 55 in.
> Seat height: 31·5 in.
> Width: 27 in.

> Ground clearance: 5 in.
> Weight: 390 lb.
> Fuel: 4 gal.
> Price: about £420

Going down the size scale, another popular production racer is the Velocette Venom Thruxton 500 which has been developed from considerable record-breaking and clubman racing experience. It has a 499 c.c. single-cylinder engine of 86 mm bore and stroke, developing 41 b.h.p. at 6,200 r.p.m.

Statistics:

> Compression ratio: 9 to 1
> Gear ratios: 4·4, 5·3, 6·97, 10·1
> Tyres: front, $3·00 \times 19$; rear, $3·25 \times 19$
> Wheelbase: 53·75 in.
> Seat height: 30·5 in.
> Width: 27·5 in.
> Ground clearance: 5·5 in.
> Weight: 375 lb.
> Fuel capacity: 4·25 gal.
> Price: £408

Races for novices are featured at a number of meetings, while most circuits are available for private practice at a small fee. For anyone doubtful of his ability, there is also a road racing school at Brands Hatch where a course of instruction and 20 laps on a 250 c.c. Ducati racer costs £9 10s.

Streamlining

General rules about clothing and machines have been noted earlier in the book, but there are some important points about streamlining.

The front wheel, with the exception of the tyre, must be clearly visible to spectators on either side. There must be no streamlining forward of the axle of the front wheel, and no streamlining farther back than the axle of the rear wheel. Normal mudguards are not considered as streamlining, but no part of the machine may project beyond the rearmost edge of the rim of the rear wheel.

It must be possible to see the whole of the rider, except for his forearms, when he is in the normal riding position from either side, from the rear and from above. And one is not allowed to dodge this rule by the use of transparent material. No part of the seat or anything to the rear of it must be more than $35\frac{1}{2}$ inches above the ground when the machine is unladen.

Exhaust pipes must not project beyond any part of the vehicle or its bodywork, and exhaust gases must not be discharged so as to raise dust or inconvenience a following rider.

Handlebars must be at least 20 inches across. Stops or other devices must be fitted to ensure a minimum clearance of $1\frac{1}{4}$ inches between handlebars and tank when on full lock, to prevent the trapping of the driver's fingers.

There must be at least 2 inches clearance between the streamlining and the extremities of the handlebars (including any attachments to them), whatever the position of the handlebars, and it must not be possible for the front wheel to touch the streamlining.

It must be possible for the motorcycle, unladen, to be inclined to an angle of 50 degrees from the vertical without any part of it, other than tyres, coming into contact with the ground. (This is, of course, because of the danger of a footrest contacting the ground when the machine is heeled over for a bend.)

But footrests, which must be rounded at the ends, must not be higher than two inches above a line through the centre of the wheels (and the rider is expected to keep his feet on them during a race, or he will be excluded).

Circuits

Where can one race in Britain? The greatest circuit of all is of course the $37\frac{3}{4}$-mile T.T. circuit with its winding roads through towns, villages and countryside, up and down Snaefell Mountain, along fast straights, round hairpin bends and over hump-backed bridges. This is the circuit by which all others are judged.

Apart from 'the island' there is a variety of circuits, from the 'natural' type ones like Oulton Park, with interesting bends and undulations, to the fast, flat and bleak airfield circuits like Silverstone. Most riders prefer the natural circuits as a better test of man and machine.

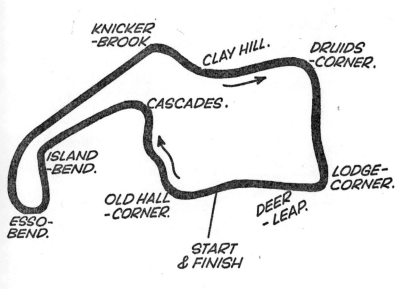

Oulton Park

I will list a few of the better-known circuits:

Oulton Park is in hilly parkland near Tarporley, Cheshire, 11 miles east of Chester. It is a 2·76-mile circuit winding up and down through woods and past a lake.

Mallory Park is a 1·4-mile course on a private estate 10 miles from Leicester near Kirkby Mallory, which is just off A47, the Hinckley–Leicester road.

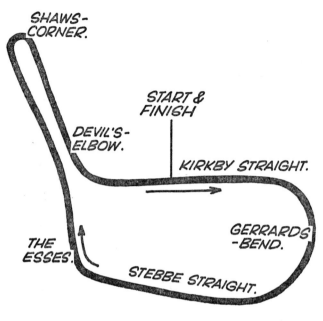

Mallory Park

Brands Hatch has two circuits, a 1¼-mile one for club events and a 2¾-mile one for major races, set in a natural amphitheatre 22 miles south-east of London beside A20, the London–Maidstone road.

Crystal Palace is London's own circuit, a 1·4-mile miniature one, yet with all types of corners save a hairpin. It is in the grounds of the old Crystal Palace at Sydenham.

Snetterton is a wartime Norfolk airfield, 10 miles north-east of Thetford off the A11 London–Norwich road, a flat 2½-mile circuit with three straights and eight bends, including a near hairpin.

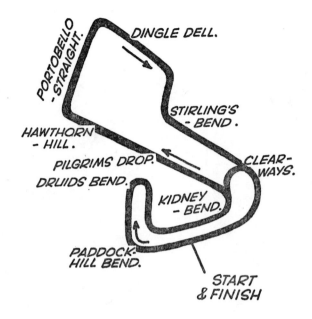

PORTOBELLO "STRAIGHT.

DINGLE DELL.

STIRLING'S - BEND.

HAWTHORN - HILL.

PILGRIMS DROP.

DRUIDS BEND.

CLEAR-WAYS.

KIDNEY - BEND.

PADDOCK-HILL BEND.

START & FINISH

Brands Hatch

Silverstone is a windy wartime airfield in Northamptonshire, 65 miles from London off the Towcester–Brackley–Banbury road. It's nearly 3 miles long, with seven straights joining eight corners.

One can see good racing at all these circuits; it is less easy to get a race at them. Meetings tend to be over-entered and one may be crowded out for a long time unless one is an established rider. The problem is how to prove oneself if one cannot get in a race. It is an old problem.

A track for road racing is normally required to be at least 16·4 feet wide and the number of drivers permitted in a solo race is calculated on the basis of one driver for every 40 inches of the

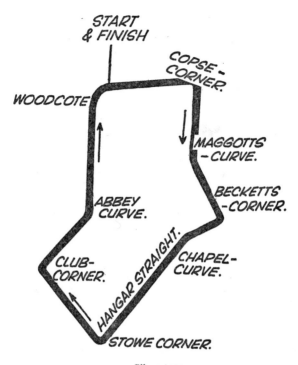

Silverstone

width of the course at its narrowest point, multiplied by one driver for every $\frac{5}{8}$ mile of the length of the course. (It sounds complicated but it works out.) Sidecars are calculated to require double the amount of space allowed for solos.

Practice

Practice has two main purposes: to enable the rider to learn the circuit and to decide on his machine's jet setting and gearing. Adopt a riding position as flat as possible, with elbows tucked in. This is an unnatural position, but since it will have to be maintained for 90 per cent of a race it is important to arrange things so that one is as comfortable as possible. Too tight leathers or badly placed controls will soon cause discomfort. A piece of sponge rubber on the fuel tank will protect the jaw.

Never lap too fast at the start of practice. It will only harm the machine. Do not be discouraged if your lap times are slower than those of others; speed will come with experience. After a few laps at a fair speed concentrate on the corners. Crawl round them, determining the best line. (Geoffrey Duke always *walked* round a new circuit before going out on his machine, in order to study the corners and any bumps.)

Go in and watch others to see how they are tackling the tricky parts of the circuit. Then try again.

Cornering

The best line is one which takes the machine through a bend in a smooth sweep. Ideally one makes a wide approach, crosses inside at the apex and makes a wide exit (though not so wide as to run on to the grass). However, road camber or loose surfacing at the verges (which should have been noted already) may require modification of this, while when overtaking slower riders one will not always be able to take the best possible line. Again, where one corner is followed immediately by another, the rider must adopt a line which will set him up for the next bend.

The rule, as always, is slow in, fast out. Brake and change down if necessary on the approach to the bend, then, as you heel over, off with the brakes and open up again smoothly. Developments in racing tyres—the latest have an angular cross-section—mean that the experts can brake as they bank if necessary, but normally braking (and gear-changing too, of course) should be done while upright and before entering the corner.

Note braking points but remember, in bad weather or when there is a strong wind behind one, to brake earlier and to be more gentle.

Though the engine can be used as a most effective brake, don't strain the transmission or run the risk of over-revving by changing down too harshly. Brakes are for using, and replacement brake-linings are cheaper than mechanical replacements.

Both brakes should be applied together. The front is the more effective brake and the harder worked. The exception is that if in trouble in a bend it is generally better to use only the rear brake to correct. Sometimes it is possible to go through a bend with the throttle still open, obtaining a moderate braking effect merely by sitting up.

One should aim never to go through a bend on a trailing throttle—the machine should be under power—and never de-clutch in a bend except for a walking-pace slow hairpin.

Do not think because you know a star rider takes a bend in top gear it follows that you can do the same, particularly if you are on a heavier and more powerful machine. Use a safe gear.

Gearing and jet setting

If the race is to be a long one make a meticulous note in practice of fuel and oil consumption in order to assess accurately when it will be necessary to call at the pits.

A tachometer (rev counter) will indicate when the gearing is wrong. If the machine is unable to reach peak revs it is over-geared; if peak revs are easily exceeded it is undergeared. Too high gearing means that the rider's lap times will be below par; too low gearing courts the risk of engine failure.

But it is unwise for the beginner in racing to alter gear-ratios until he has acquired familiarity with a circuit and the ability to assess his performance accurately.

Carburettor settings must be such that one can rely on the engine firing first time at the start and giving maximum acceleration afterwards. Since a too weak mixture may cause the engine to overheat and lose power, and may burn out plugs and valves, it is better to err, if at all, on the side of a too rich mixture.

The plug or plugs will give an indication of the state of the mixture. Kill the engine with the magneto switch, simultaneously declutching as you come in from practice. Provided correct plugs are fitted, dry whitish points will indicate a weak mixture, requiring an increase in the jet size. Black, sooty points indicate a rich one, requiring a reduction in the jet size. They *should* be a moist-looking dark grey.

Plugs should be as hard as is necessary to stand up to the conditions of the race. Too hard plugs tend to oil up, and so it is a good plan to be armed with a plug one grade softer in case this happens.

At the end of a long practice period it is a good plan to drain and change the oil, but do not attempt last-minute modifications of a major nature. Better by far to leave well alone; content yourself with adjusting chains, checking the contact-breaker gap and tightening all nuts which may have been loosened by vibration. For assured starting, plugs must be clean and in good condition, and ignition setting must be just right—too much advance may mean kick-back and it is better to have the ignition a shade retarded.

Tyre pressures should be adjusted to the nature of the surface. They are usually of the order of 25 to 28 lb. per sq. in. Wheels should be balanced.

Competition numbers will already have been painted. The usual colours required are:

Solo machines up to 50 c.c., white plates, black numbers,

100 c.c. to 125 c.c., black with white numbers,

Over 125 c.c. to 250 c.c., green with white numbers,

Over 250 c.c. to 350 c.c., blue with white numbers,

Over 350 c.c. to 1,000 c.c., yellow with black numbers.

On a streamlined machine it is permissible to paint numbers on the streamlining instead of on plates.

Starting

In some races (including the T.T.s) competitors are started singly or in pairs from a starting line, but in most races all riders are started together from a grid, the positions on the grid having been decided by lap times in practice. (The fastest riders get the front positions.) Occasionally, though, positions may be decided by lot or by a system of seeding. In timing the results it is assumed that all riders started from the starting line and the fact that the riders at the front of the grid had several yards advantage over the men at the back is ignored.

Usually riders line up with engines dead and push-start their machines. They must start unaided. At a signal machines are pushed out on to the grid. Here check that petrol is switched on and the carburettor full. (Norman Surtees admits to having forgotten to switch on in his first road race, a novices meeting at Oulton Park, but he still finished fourth and won his next event.)

Oil should be warm. Some riders pre-heat it over a portable stove (but remember to take the cap off the can first). If the oil is cold and viscous it means taking things easy in the early stages of the race, or there is a danger of burnt valve-seats and broken piston-rings.

Pull goggles down, select bottom gear, pull the machine backwards on to compression and free the clutch. Be ready to push, or adopt the technique of pushing as soon as the starter's flag goes up, while keeping the model still by holding on to the front brake with the right hand. This cuts out the need to gather oneself to start pushing when the flag comes down; the weight is already behind the machine and it is only necessary to release the brake.

Either way, keep your eyes on the starter and as soon as the flag begins to fall start to run and push. Run three or four steps (allow six in wet weather or the exertion may cause a slip). In with the clutch, at the same time leaping on board sidesaddle; the nodel should fire. Mind any riders who may be unable to start. If your machine has not started don't panic. Push again. Do not use too much throttle or you may over-flood the carburettor.

Now you're away; out with the clutch again momentarily to build up revs. Clutch in again and pick a path through the pack. Be ready to swing into the astride position; you must be astride before reaching peak revs in bottom gear. Once astride, assume the crouch position, tuck in the elbows, shrink behind the fairing

Production racer, static. A Velocette Venom Thruxton, winner of many races

Production racer, at speed. A Triumph Bonneville racing at Barcelona

Scooter sport—British scooterists travel all over Europe on rallies.
Here riders from Britain on Vespa Gran Sport machines are taking
part in a test on Germany's famous, tortuous Nurburgring

Gymkhana—They are a long way removed from road racing but light-
hearted tests like this (at a Leamington Spa Gymkhana Championship)
are all part of motorcycle sport

and up through the gears. Some experts do not use the clutch to change up. With the close-ratio gearboxes of a racing machine this is quite practicable and saves a movement, but it is not a technique to be recommended to the novice.

Be prepared to change down and brake for the first bend. Remember that features of a circuit can change between practice and race; for instance, a tree or gateway noted as a braking point may now be obscured by spectators.

Tactics
Some riders let others set the pace, making their way to the front only in the closing stages of a race. Derek Minter frequently came from the back of the field to win. Others like to get in front at the start and stay there. This was John Surtees' technique; it is the best one for most riders.

When a machine is not up to the power of others, or has been overgeared, top riders often indulge in slipstreaming, tucking in behind a faster man and letting him draw them along. This is not to be recommended unless you are very skilled and you know the man from whom you are getting the 'tow' is equally skilled, for if he makes a mistake, does something foolish or leads you into an error of judgment on a bend, it will be extremely difficult to avoid an accident. It is hard to shake off a rider who slipstreams you; weaving may do it but it cuts speed.

In long-distance races riders try various—perfectly legitimate— tricks to crush opposition, such as pressing another man until his machine blows up or pretending that one's own machine lacks power, but these cannot be resorted to in short events.

If it looks like raining it is wise to try to achieve a commanding lead before it starts, particularly if riders have been started at intervals, for the race will slow down when the rain arrives.

If you are well in front do not keep going faster, just to try to set a lap record to show off. This may break the bike quite un- necessarily. The experts' maxim is 'Win at the slowest possible speed'. Never go faster than is necessary to win.

A notice which I have seen in the pits at Cadwell Park said:

F

WARNING

There are no medals for falling off.
Wild driving is your sure ticket for no return.

If you can afford to ease up, spare the engine not yourself.
Change up earlier, brake less fiercely. If you need to sit up for a
rest try to do it when the wind is behind you.

Pit Stops

Pit stops are for refuelling. They are not tea breaks, nor occasions
for a chat about the race. Have a trustworthy helper. He should
begin refuelling the moment you stop (in bottom gear). There
should be a drink ready for you and a spare pair of goggles in
case your first pair have become bespattered by oil and dust.

Pull the machine back on to compression and free the clutch
as the topping-up process nears its end; all this should have been
rehearsed many times, so that words are unnecessary.

Take a quick look to make sure no oil has got on to footrests,
brake pedal or tyres, check that the oil tank is properly shut and
get out again. Less than half a minute should have passed.

Signals from your pit attendant should consist of only two
figures—the first your position in the race, the second the time in
seconds, plus or minus, separating you from the next man.

Official flag signals are the same as given in the last chapter. So
are regulations about the finish and results.

Road races are hardly ever stopped prematurely (it did happen
in a downpour in the 1954 Senior T.T. and enthusiasts are still
arguing about that decision). If stopped before half-distance the
race becomes null and void; if stopped later the stewards decide
the results, but a race is virtually never re-run.

Women in road racing

I must admit that there is strong prejudice against women in
road racing. In recent years I can think of only three who have
competed with any success.

Margo Pearson, a redhead from Erdington, Birmingham, began in trials at the age of seventeen, switched to racing on a 125 c.c. Spanish Montesa.

Pat Wise, an Addlestone, Surrey, housewife, was Eric Oliver's sidecar passenger in the 1958 T.T. (they came tenth). After that she raced a man-sized 500 c.c. Velocette Venom and a 350 c.c. Manx Norton at Silverstone and Oulton Park.

The third girl, who made a considerable dent in masculine prejudice in 1962 when she became the first woman to ride in a T.T. race (as opposed to acting as a sidecar passenger), was blonde Beryl Swain, wife of a Walthamstow garage owner. After heavy eating to reach the nine-stone minimum weight—she was no Amazon—she rode her Italian Itom into twenty-second place (out of thirty-three starters) in the 50 c.c. race, despite being reduced to the two lowest gears. (Her speed was 48·33 m.p.h. against winner Ernst Degner's 75·12 m.p.h.)

Since then women have been barred from international events —though they can still compete up to national level.

So it is possible for girls to go road racing—but they have got to be very determined and prepared to meet opposition.

Grass-track racing

Grass-track racing might be described as the poor man's road racing. It also serves as a nursery for road racers; many top riders have begun on grass courses laid out in fields, among them sidecar experts Chris Vincent and Bill Boddice. Only in 1962 did grass-track achieve the dignity of an A.C.U. championship like trialling, scrambling and road racing.

Yet it has its own greats, outstanding among them being bespectacled Alf Hagon of Leyton, Essex, who has been known to win 278 races in a year! Alf, one of the greatest all-rounders in motorcycling, is an ex-speedway rider, and some grass-track meetings are virtually speedways on grass. The riders broadside speedway machines round tight bends on slippery grass instead of cinders, the nearside foot thrust out in speedway style.

Other circuits are longer—though rarely more than a mile—and for these the technique is more orthodox.

Machines need something of the qualities of both road racers and of scramblers. The majority are home-made specials, built from a variety of motorcycles. Alf Hagon has made seventy different machines, a great many for other riders.

Grass-track racing tends to be a more sociable, clubby form of sport than road racing. The minimum width of a grass track is 25 feet, on which not more than four riders are permitted to start in a solo scratch race. The number of riders may be increased by one for every extra 3 feet of width. (For three-wheelers the number is half that permitted for solo races.)

Every part of the course to which spectators have access has to be protected by a safety fence of wood, turves or wire, or (as is more usual) by a system of wide safety spaces and rope-linked posts.

Incidentally the grass of a grass track seldom lasts out a season!

10

Sprinting

SPRINTING (which includes record-breaking) was one of the earliest motorcycle sports. Record attempts were being made in 1902. It lost favour in the 'twenties as motor-age restrictions grew and flat courses with room for pulling up became more difficult to find, but after the war Britain had 300 surplus airfields, many of them ideal for sprinting.

Sprinting began to grow in popularity again, and continues to grow. There are frequent meetings on Saturdays between March and October.

Len Cole, founder of the National Sprint Association, says, 'Sprinting has one great advantage; whatever your standard you have an equal share of the limelight with the top men, whereas in road racing you can get lost in the pack and never be seen.'

What does it involve? Very simply, covering a short set distance in the quickest possible time. It is really an acceleration test. The most popular distance is 440 yards—a quarter of a mile.

At some meetings the riders are launched one at a time, but the National Sprint Association are encouraging promoters to arrange for them to go off in pairs. This obvious competition creates more excitement for spectators and can turn a financial flop into a money-maker. When records are at stake competitors make two runs, one in either direction. A time limit of 30 minutes is set for completion of the two runs and no alterations to the machine are permitted in between, other than the changing of plugs and of tyres or wheels (and the replacements must be identical to those originally fitted).

Sprint entries are in classes governed by engine capacity, and whether or not a supercharger is fitted has no bearing on the matter.

The speeds that are reached? On a 440-yards course the 500 c.c. to 1,000 c.c. machines cross the finishing line at between 105 and 140 m.p.h. and average about 80 m.p.h. In one-kilometre sprints, the most popular distance for world-record attempts, machines reach 145 to 175 m.p.h.

Sprint machines

Sprinting is still a Cinderella sport. Membership of the National Sprint Association (which also caters for car sprint-racing) is around 800, of which only about 200 are active, competing members.

To be successful in sprints probably required more mechanical and engineering knowledge than any other branch of the sport—paddocks at spring meetings are the busiest to be seen anywhere. For the keen, ambitious competitor sprinting can be costly, there being very few restrictions on the work which may be done to a machine. The man in search of records can spend a small fortune on buying the lightest, finest, light-alloy components. Nitro-methane fuels cost £14 per gallon, which is expensive even for a drink with a kick, and sprint machines can gulp fuel like veteran topers. A common nitro-methanol mix costs £2 10s. per gallon.

Yet for the clubman sprinting can also be the cheapest of sports, for it is not possible to buy a ready-made specialist sprint special as one can buy scramblers, trials bikes and road racers. Sprinting is for 'specials', normal production machines doctored to achieve explosive acceleration.

What are the basic requirements?

Firstly comes *streamlining*, used extensively even in 'quarters'. Polished aluminium is most esteemed; fibre-glass the most used.

Then *tyres*. A 'slick' on the rear wheel is essential. This is a treadless tyre, such a tyre providing more contact with the ground (sprinters do not ride on soft tyres, though). The surge of acceleration of a big sprint special would cause it to spin off without a slick.

Then comes *gearing*. The choice of the correct gearing is perhaps the greatest art in sprinting, particularly in a quarter where there is no time to compensate for errors. (From the time the machine actuates the timing-gear at the start of a run it will take no more than 10 to 20 seconds, depending on class, to cross the line.)

There are two schools of thought as to the number of gear-changes needed in a sprint. Many big machines have utilized four gears to win quarters, yet Alf Hagon has won quarters and broken records on an ultra-light low-built 649 c.c. Triumph, using only a two-gear box.

Wheelbases are lengthened, bringing weight forward to hold the front wheel down on take-off. Machines are stripped and perforated to achieve lightness. Stamina is unimportant; the machine has not got to survive the many laps and gear-changes of a road race, just to be able to travel fast over a short, flat course. And fuel may be laced with nitro-methane, which releases oxygen and creates a sort of chemical supercharging.

When it comes to riding a sprint bike a fast getaway is of paramount importance. Len Cole says, 'A fast getaway depends on lightness in man and machine, a lot of power and just enough wheelspin.'

Ex-speedway men like Alf Hagon seem to take naturally to sprinting; they know exactly how much throttle to give at the start.

'Nero'

'Father' of Britain's post-war sprinting boom was George Brown, a Stevenage, Herts, motorcycle dealer who has broken more records than any other rider in the country and succeeded in making nonsense of an F.I.M. age-limit of 55 on world-record bids.

Among his records were 189·33 m.p.h. for the solo flying

quarter-mile and 158·45 m.p.h. for the sidecar flying kilometre. A quick look at his two most famous machines shows what can be done to and with standard production machines. They were named Nero and Super Nero and started life as 998 c.c. Vincents. (Brown used to be a test rider for the firm.)

The original Nero was lightened to 320 lb., less than many road-going 250 c.c. machines, and fed on nitro. Eventually it was discarded as obsolete. 'Old Nero was a bit brutal at certain speeds and took a lot of handling,' said Brown. Then he built Super Nero.

Again he used a 998 c.c. Vincent. First the wheelbase was stretched to a lengthy 61 inches to keep the front end from rearing on the start-line. The frame was also lowered. Then a big Shorrocks supercharger, capable of giving a boost of 12¾ lb. pressure, was fitted between gearbox, rear cylinder and rear tyre. Because of the supercharger, compression ratio was dropped from 13 to 1 to 8 to 1 but the ignition advance was increased. An S.U. carburettor of 2-inch bore was fitted to deliver the methanol fuel.

An Avon slick tyre was fitted at the rear on an 18-inch light-alloy rim. At the front a $2·75 \times 19$ racing tyre was installed on a wheel from an A.J.S. 7R.

Everything possible was perforated with a power drill to lighten weight which, despite the 30 lb. supercharger, was brought down to 320 lb.

Brown's ambition was to become the first man to beat 200 m.p.h. on a motorcycle in Britain. But that honour was to go to Alf Hagon on his 1,260 c.c. Hagon-JAP. He was also the first to break into 10 seconds for the standing start quarter-mile sprint under world record conditions (which demand the mean of consecutive runs in opposite directions).

Brown's other dream was of taking the world speed record. Since there is nowhere in Britain where such a speed can be attempted he planned to go to Lake Eyre in South Australia where Donald Campbell took his Bluebird car. But today it seems unlikely that any Briton can obtain the facilities to improve on the 245·67 m.p.h. for the flying mile set up in 1966 by Bob Leppan of

Detroit with a fully-streamlined projectile powered by two 649 c.c. Trimph Bonneville engines. (Though it is interesting that Dennis Norman, a Hemel Hempstead motor engineer, has been sprinting a similarly-engined machine.)

Record-breaking attempts on this scale are obviously expensive. Brown reckons major record bids in the past have cost him £200 to £300 each, even after financial aid from tyre and oil companies, and the trip to Australia (including three months there tuning and experimenting) could cost £7,000.

Sprint courses
Britain's centre for record-breaking attempts is Elvington airfield in Yorkshire where, at weekend meetings, a score of records have been known to fall. Other sprint courses are also mainly airfield ones—Totcliffe, Debden, Duxford and Bassingbourne, but the seaside course at Blackpool is also popular.

Hill climbing
Hill climbing is only sprinting uphill, though some hills have tricky bends. Oldest and most famous course in the country is Shelsley Walsh between Worcester and Tenbury, off B4204. It is 1,000 yards long with a steepest gradient of 1 in 6·26.

II

Scooters

SCOOTER sport has been the fastest-growing branch of motorized two-wheel sport. One reason is simple: it is the cheapest.

Scooters are not a recent invention. They were popular just after the First World War, though not on the same scale as today. Present-day scootering began after the Second World War with Corgis, developed from the folding machines used by para-troopers, which were followed by the Vespas and Lambrettas from Italy. On the Continent scootering was soon a craze, and more slowly it was taken up in Britain.

At first scooters were looked upon merely as cheap runabouts, but as engines, bodies and performances improved it was realized they could be used for sporting purposes.

P. James Agg, managing director of Lambretta Concessionaires, said: 'Motorcyclists, who used to look upon scooter entries with disfavour, have grown to admire the performance of both riders and machines.'

Scooter sport has its own stars in men like Neville Frost of Watford, champion scooterist of 1969, when he won the Tour of Britain on a 125 c.c. machine.

Today the scooterist probably has as big a programme of events open to him between May and October as any other two-wheel rider.

There are about 200 scooter clubs with an average of forty to fifty members each, nearly all running rallies, navigation and driving tests, obstacle races and the like. Some are one-make-only clubs (for Lambretta and Vespa owners, mainly); others cater for owners of all makes of scooter.

Scooter rallies
Among the bigger events is the Isle of Man Scooter Rally in which entrants set out from various points and converge on Liverpool for a boat to the island, where they spend a week in various tests and gymkhana events, plus a run on the T.T. course. The Tour of Britain, the scooterists' Monte Carlo, has involved an 836-mile ride from Leicester through Yorkshire dales to the Lake District. There is also the Cambrian Two-Day Event which takes riders round Wales.

There are rallies abroad too, In an international Lambretta run to Istanbul, 174 red, yellow, orange and blue scooters converged on Trieste from many European countries, then headed over the mountains out of Yugoslavia and along shocking roads through Greece at an average of 40 m.p.h. The British riders covered 3,500 miles on this trip.

There have been road races for scooters. There are scooter scrambles (or Scootacross) and there are scooter trials.

There are four main classes in scooter events: under 100 c.c., 101 to 150 c.c., 151 to 200 c.c., and over 200 c.c. There are also scooter sidecar events.

Definition of a scooter
How does a scooter differ from an ultra-lightweight motorcycle? Most people would define a scooter as being a machine on which the rider can sit on a seat with an open space in front of it for his legs, without being astride a frame.

The definition of a scooter for the purposes of sport goes rather further. The A.C.U. rule that the minimum size of the space forward of the seat must be 25 centimetres along a parallel line projected from the top of the seat towards the steering column and 25 centimetres downwards from that line. This space, which may reduce to 10 cm. long at the base, must be clear at all times of any obstruction.

The rim diameter of the wheels must not exceed 16 inches. The scooter must have a kick-starter or an automatic starting device and must have a body and legshields in the form of an apron not less than 40 cm in width and length. Footrests must be of the platform type and at least 30 centimetres long.

Types of scooters

Perhaps the most competitive sporting scooter is the *Lambretta Grand Prix* 198 c.c. machine introduced in 1969. Styled by Bertone, the Italian car stylist, it is lower, narrower and more powerful than its predecessors.

Its two-stroke, single-cylinder four-speed engine develops 11·7 b.h.p. at 6,200 r.p.m., which gives it a top speed of 68·8 m.p.h., a cruising speed of 46·8 m.p.h. and a quarter-mile acceleration time of 21·1 seconds. Fuel consumption is just over 70 m.p.g. and the brakes are disc at the front and drum at the rear.

Statistics:

> Compression ratio: 7·3 to 1
> Gear ratios: 5·22, 6·79, 9·13, 13·05
> Tyres: $3·50 \times 10$
> Length: 70·8 in.
> Width: 26·8 in.
> Seat height: 30·39 in.
> Weight: 271 lb.
> Fuel capacity: 1·78 gal.
> Price: £243

There is also a 148 c.c. Grand Prix model with a top speed of 63 m.p.h., a cruising speed of 42 m.p.h. and a fuel consumption of 87 m.p.g. which sells at £204.

But it is not necessarily the newest and best machine that wins competitions. Chuck Swennel, a Croydon toolmaker, won the 126 to 250 c.c. class in the 24-hour, 600 miles National Rally of 1969 on an eight-year-old scooter with more than 100,000 miles on the clock.

For grass track events, which have rather superseded scrambles in popularity among scooterists, it is usual to acquire an old scooter which is stripped of all but essentials so that it looks little like a road-going scooter save for the obligatory space in the frame where a motorcycle would have its engine.

What can be removed and done to machines has varied from club to club in the past but the Federation of British Scooter Clubs has now devised general rules applicable to scooters to supplement the A.C.U.'s General Competition Rules.

12

Sidecar Sport

SIDECAR events are certainly spectacular to watch, but why do people choose to drive sidecar combinations in sporting events, rather than solo machines? According to Mike Cole, a veteran of the British Sporting Sidecar Association: 'Most solo riders think sidecar boys are mad—and vice versa. I started out as a solo rider, then tried my hand with a sidecar. After the first go I wanted to pack it in; the sidecar is a more complicated machine to handle. But once I had mastered it I would never go back to the solo machine. And there are other soloists who are "going sidecar".

'The appeal of sidecar sport so far as I am concerned is mainly that there is more skill in it. You have to act as a team with your passenger. For the soloist it's just "lean and turn" for all corners. The sidecar rider has to open his throttle going into left-handers and shut it down when taking right-handers, because the bike is on the right and so is the drive. Take a left-hander too fast and the chair-wheel will come off the ground. Take a right-hander too fast and the machine's rear wheel is likely to come up. That's why the control of the throttle has to be exact in sidecar racing.

'Another appeal the sidecar world offers is that the social side is better than the soloist's. Being a minority group, all the sidecar enthusiasts know each other and there is more spirit in our game, I think.'

Classes
Sidecar events may be divided into the following classes:

Class	Minimum engine capacity in c.c.	Maximum engine capacity in c.c.
Category B (1, 2 and 3)		
350	——	350
500	350	500
750	500	750
1000	750	1000
1300	1000	1300
Category B (4)		
125	——	125
250	125	250

It will be noted that the second category caters for scooters fitted with sidecars. The first also includes cyclecars.

The most popular form of sidecar sport in this country is scrambling, followed closely by trials riding. Road racing has a limited following, due to the high cost of a chance of success.

Road racing
The outfits of the top men in road racing cost around £1,000 and are not available 'over the counter'. And though enthusiasts can build and fit their own 'chairs' to production machines they cannot compete on equal terms.

Top machine in sidecar racing has for several years been the German B.M.W. (for Bavarian Motor Works). The horizontally opposed twin-cylinder engine is ideal for the purpose, and handled by men like Max Deubel of Cologne and his passenger, Emil Hoerner, B.M.W.s have won the world-championship crown regularly since 1954. The Germans, as a race, are sidecar enthusiasts.

However, Chris Vincent, a B.S.A. driver, has been a consistent winner in British races on a standard production machine, and in clubman's events many of the big British-made machines will suffice.

The Watsonian firm used to make a racing sidecar based on the design of a 'chair' used by ex-world champion Eric Oliver (greatest of all sidecar racers in his heyday) in sprint events.

It had a platform of wood faced with light alloy and an unsprung wheel with a light-alloy rim taking a $3 \cdot 50 \times 12$ in. Dunlop racing tyre. There was a streamlined glass-fibre mudguard and nose. The body-weight was 68 lb. and Watsonian supplied fittings for attaching it to a Manx Norton, a Matchless G50 or a B.M.W.

However, production has now ended and for all forms of sidecar sport competitors have to build their own 'chairs' or have them made to order.

Building a sidecar

When building or converting a sidecar combination for racing (which includes scrambling) certain regulations must be observed.

The three road wheels, which may be disposed to give either two or three tracks, must each be at least 16 inches in diameter, measured over the outside of the tyre. (This does not apply to scooters.) One of the wheels may be replaced by two wheels, provided the distance between the vertical centre lines of these two wheels does not exceed 8 inches. The wheel track, or lateral distance between tracks, must be at least 32 inches. There must be independently operated brakes on at least two wheels.

The position of the engine is optional, and the engine may drive one or more road wheels.

The provision of coachwork or streamlining is also optional, but the sidecar must have accommodation for one or more passengers, who must be completely protected from the road wheels and drive, either by mudguarding or some other means.

If streamlining is fitted the driver must be able to get on and off and drive the machine without having to remove any part of the streamlining. The front of the streamlining must not project beyond the front tyre by more than 4 inches. At the back it must not project more than a foot beyond the rear tyre. The height above the ground of the rear part of the streamlining and of the

Rallying—For many rallies map-reading skill as well as riding skill is needed. Competitors in a Kent event raise a point with a marshal before the start

Sidecar racing—Emil Hoerner has his shoulder scraping the ground as he balances the B.M.W. outfit of world champion Max Deubel on a bend. (The sidecar is mounted Continental fashion on the offside of the machine)

Machine preparation—
Checking contact breaker
points gap with a feeler
gauge

Machine preparation—
Brake cables must be
lubricated regularly

saddle and other components must not exceed 35½ inches when the motorcycle is unladen, and there must be at least 2 inches between the streamlining and the handlebars (including any attachments), whatever the position of the handlebars.

In trials, and other competitions apart from races, the sidecar body must be covered by a skin of either metal or 'some other substantial material' (such as fibre-glass).

The sidecar must be at least 54 inches long from nose to tail and the cockpit must be at least 15 inches wide at the seat position, Panels must enclose the sides of the body completely and not be less than 5 inches deep at any point. The height of the body at the apex of the dashboard position must be at least 15 inches and from this point forwards the nose must be completely covered and at least 18 inches long.

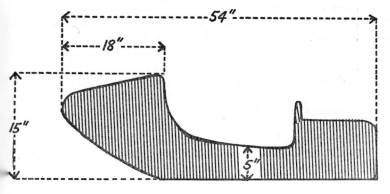

Trials sidecar

In other words, the sidecar must be a proper one, not a skeleton. Note that these measurements are minimum ones; there is no restriction on how much bigger the 'chair' may be.

The normal seating position must be in the cockpit and there must be provision for a proper seat and backrest, though they may be removed for competitions. Grab-rails, handles and straps can be fitted according to the designer's own ideas.

G

Toe-in

A bike and sidecar cannot just be joined together in parallel fashion. There is road camber to be allowed for and the fact that as propulsion comes from the rear wheel of the machine it exerts a drag to the left. To counter the splaying-out effect when on the road the sidecar wheel must 'toe-in' towards the machine.

Toe-in can be checked (on level ground) by the use of two straight boards. Place one alongside the two wheels of the bike—which should be in line. Place the other alongside the sidecar wheel. The distance between the boards at the front wheel of the motorcycle should be about $1\frac{1}{2}$ inches less than at the rear.

The motorcycle may be vertical or lean out slightly from the sidecar, but should never be inclined towards it. It should also be noted that if the sidecar wheel is mounted too far forward the steering will be heavy; if it is mounted too far back drag will be increased. All in all the attachment of a sidecar requires expert knowledge; it is not possible to take a sidecar from one machine and fit it to a different make without some adjustments.

If the outfit is correctly aligned it should steer 'hands off'.

Handling a combination

Driving a combination requires an entirely different technique from riding a solo. Instead of leaning into a bend one has to *steer* round, using the handlebars like a tiller. At the same time, as Mike Cole says, one must accelerate on a left-hander to make the machine run round the 'chair'; ease the throttle on a right-hander to let the sidecar come round the machine.

It is useful practice to drive in and out between imaginary posts, alternately opening up as one swings left and throttling back as one turns right, mastering the handling and how to bring down a wheel if it lifts.

Then one must practise with one's passenger. On left-handers his job is to lean out to the left to keep that wheel down; on right-handers he puts his weight over the rear wheel. At speed, if he moves out too soon he will cost you revs and slow you; too late and the outfit will capsize. Practice is needed until the minds of driver and passenger are as one.

Try not to lose the passenger overboard. Apart from making for ill-feeling, the regulations say that during a race the passenger must be 'effectively and continuously carried on the vehicle in the place provided for him'. He is allowed to leave his seat only at the start, on bends and when the motorcycle is stationary. The penalty for breaking this rule is exclusion.

A sprint-race passenger has a particularly difficult time because of the shattering acceleration and the shortness of the run. He has got to weight the rear wheel at the start to prevent it spinning, then get out of the way behind the fairing while the outfit roars for the line. The trick is to make the move to the 'chair' during the driver's first gear-change; after that infinitesimal pause it will be virtually impossible due to the acceleration.

The passenger

Kitted out, a passenger must weigh at least 9 stone 6 lb.; jockeys and other midgets are therefore barred. Ideally the passenger should be less than 11 stone. An all-in wrestler is not recommended; he may hold the outfit on the road but will be costly in speed and pulling power.

A passenger's role is ideal for someone who is keen on the sport but does not have the skill to make the grade as a rider, or the cash to buy a machine. In fact many top passengers who have helped win innumerable races could hardly drive an outfit themselves. (Incidentally, there have been some excellent girl passengers.)

Passengers are allowed to wear plimsolls to assist them in keeping a foothold. Ear-plugs are also recommended.

In some events, particularly sprinting, ballast is allowed instead of a passenger. The ballast must consist of a single object weighing at least 132 lb. and fixed to the passenger seat. Remember that while an inanimate lump of lead will not break the streamlining, will not fall overboard (if properly fixed) and will not make tiresome complaints about the driving, it cannot climb about to help the driver.

13

In the Workshop

THERE is a popular belief among laymen that an expert tuner can take a standard motorcycle, breathe on it in some magical way and within half an hour give it an extra 10 m.p.h. to make it the fastest machine of its kind in the country. This is completely false.

It is true that a few adjustments may bring an off-song machine back to the standard of performance it should have, but tinkering will not improve performance beyond the standard, nor can it bring back the performance of a worn-out engine.

Indeed tinkering, without a sound plan behind it, is far more likely to do harm than good, for it is impossible to alter one aspect of an engine without affecting the machine in other directions, and one may introduce most undesirable characteristics.

To improve the performance of a motorcycle materially major modifications are needed, and these are not to be attempted without an overall plan, and a clear understanding of what one is doing and why one is doing it.

It is obvious that an increase in the top speed of a standard machine should be made only if braking is improved to match it. Raising of the speed may also introduce handling problems and engine imbalance. One cannot slap on a bigger carburettor unrelated to the shape and size of ports and valves. Reckless perforating of frame and moving parts to lighten weight can seriously weaken the strength of the machine, while the unthinking addition of streamlining can cut off air to engine and crankcase.

Racing conversions, offered by some manufacturers and professional tuners, recognize and allow for the difficulties. (Incidentally, if a conversion is carried out to a roadgoing machine the insurance company should be notified.) It is not within the scope of this book to offer a treatise on thermodynamics and finer points of tuning, which involve knowledge of various rules and formulae. For this I recommend the reader to P. E. Irving's *Tuning for Speed* (Temple Press Ltd.) or *Speed and how to obtain it* by the staff of *The Motor Cycle* (Butterworth), which cost 21*s*. and 8*s*. 6*d*. respectively.

But anyone other than a top-flight competitor is well advised to concentrate merely on keeping his machine at the peak of its efficiency without making major changes.

Workshop equipment

Keen sportsmen will want a home workshop of some sort, even if a modest one; a bench in the garage will serve.

Buy good tools; cheap ones bend and become distorted and may damage parts. Always hang them up; never leave them loose on a bench. First requirements are spanners, a set of open-ended ones for general purposes, box-spanners which bear on all six flats of a nut instead of just two for stubborn ones and ring-spanners for hard-to-reach ones. Except in an emergency, adjustable spanners should be shunned like motorists with dancing dolls in the windscreen. They can be almost guaranteed to round the squared flats of a nut.

A vice, a hacksaw, pliers with a wirecutting device, a hammer and cold-chisel, files, a scraper and a soldering iron will also be needed.

Jam jars for keeping small parts in, tins for holding drained oil and trays for petrol to wash parts in, a waste bin and some non-fluffy rags and a paintbrush for wiping and dusting are other essentials.

A power drill is a good buy if it can be afforded, for it will performs a variety of functions, including working a lathe.

For lighting purposes a fluorescent tube is preferable to a bulb over the bench, because it gives a more even light. Since motorcycle engines are likely to be run in the workshop, look to the ventilation. Carbon monoxide exhaust fumes can kill.

Running in

A new engine or piston must be run in before any tuning can be done. A thousand miles is the normal running-in mileage during which the engine should not be stressed. For the first 250 miles no more than quarter throttle should be used (the twist grip can be marked to indicate this). Then the oil should be changed to get rid of minute particles of metal.

After this the speed can be worked up progressively. Running in is not accomplished by riding slowly until 1,000 miles has been covered and then going out and thrashing the machine. The idea is to increase speeds gradually over the running-in period, beginning with short bursts which may gradually get longer and harder.

Running in need not be a particularly tedious process. A big bike may be taken up to 60 m.p.h. quite early on, provided it is for a short period and on a downhill or level stretch. The main consideration is to avoid letting the engine labour. Running in is well worth while.

General maintenance

Routine checks and servicing of the machine should be carried out on a mileage basis. The bike should be cleaned, nuts tightened, brakes adjusted, frayed cables replaced and chains checked and lubricated regularly.

Do not let cylinder barrel fins become caked with dirt; this reduces the cooling. But do not polish the fins either. A black surface radiates heat better than a bright one.

Grease-nipples should be given regular attention with the specified grade of grease, oil reservoirs topped up, but not over-filled, with the correct grades of oil (two-stroke engines being particularly exacting in their requirements). Keep filters clean so that oil flow is not restricted.

Tyres should be kept normally to the makers' recommended

pressures, stones removed immediately they are spotted and caps kept on the valves.

Plugs and contact-breaker points should be kept clean and correctly gapped, batteries topped up with distilled water to a level just covering the plates and terminals kept free from corrosion.

A suggested frequency for these operations is often given in the makers' manuals.

Getting the best performance

Going a stage further, what can be done to bring a used machine to the peak of its performance?

First, the engine. The fuel tank will have to be removed to gain access, which provides an opportunity to clean the tank, filters and taps and check for leaks. The carburettor will also have to be disconnected and should be dismantled. Wash out the float-chamber and check the slide for wear.

Dismantle the engine completely, watching for telltale oil leaks and discarding worn nuts, bolts and other parts. Engines must be reliable if one is to succeed in sport.

Remove the cylinder head and barrel, marking the piston (not on a bearing surface of course) so that it can be replaced in the same position. Check all parts for cracks. Clean the barrel inside and out, removing carbon from the upper part of the bore with a slip of wood and a brush, and polish the bore with metal polish.

Polish the piston head and skirt to a mirror finish, but be careful not to alter the contours. Examine the piston rings for bright spots, indicating contact with the bore. If they are bright they will need filing to increase the gap; if they are discoloured the gap is too big, meaning inefficiency and the likelihood of ring breakage, and they should be replaced.

On a two-stroke polish the inlet port, being careful not to alter its shape. On a four-stroke examine the valves and remove any pitting by grinding in the seating area with as fine a grade of paste as practicable. (A wooden-handled rubber suction-cup tool can be obtained for the purpose.)

The crankcase should be removed and its components, including bearings, washed in petrol. Polish inside the crankcase, making sure oilways are not blocked. Rotate the flywheel assembly to discover tight spots, and polish. Also polish connecting-rods and camshafts.

When reassembling a detachable-head engine see that the gasket's inner edge merges with the contour inside the head and does not project.

See that sparking plugs are of the correct reach, whatever grade of plug is being used. (Road racing with prolonged use of high speed requires a hard plug; in scrambling, where maximum speed is not maintained for so long, a softer one can be used and in trials a still softer grade.) Make sure that the lead is attached firmly to the plug terminal; many races, particularly scrambles, have been lost through leads coming adrift.

After reassembly and running the machine for some miles tighten up the fixing bolts when the engine is cool, to cope with settling.

It is not usually practicable to rebore a badly worn engine for use in sport, because reboring will normally increase the capacity to an extent which will put the machine into a bigger class.

Check over all other parts of the machine. The steering should be checked by supporting the frame on a box so that the front wheel is in the air and twisting the forks. If there is play the head bearings may be tightened by two locknuts at the top of the steering column, but do not overtighten. If the steering is rough unscrew the nuts, dismantle the head and replace the cups and balls.

Spin the wheel to check that it is running true. If the spokes are touched with a spanner as the wheel revolves they will emit musical notes. Any spokes that give out different notes are in need of tension adjustment—a job best left to a specialist. An unbalanced wheel can be corrected by wrapping lead around spokes on the light side.

Brakes are vitally important. *The Highway Code* regards a stopping distance of 45 ft. from 30 m.p.h. to be satisfactory. The rider should not. Worn brake-linings may be skimmed to improve efficiency, but if linings are badly worn detach the brake-shoes and take them to a dealer to get replacement linings.

Racing-type magnetos should be overhauled by the manufacturer. The gearbox can generally be left alone unless trouble is suspected. Then dismantle and check the gears for missing teeth, chipped and pitted faces.

Chains should be removed for cleaning and checking. Do not put new links in a worn chain, always replace the entire chain, particularly if it has become badly elongated. The chain should be fastened by rivets, not by a connector. When examining the chain look also at sprockets for worn teeth.

Clean inside the exhaust pipe to ensure that gases are not restricted.

Modifications

Anyone planning to modify a machine is recommended first to study the manual for it and then to seek the advice of the manufacturer. The factory staff know more about the model and what can be done to it than anyone; they will be interested in any brainwaves for improving its performance, but will also be able to warn of pitfalls. They have seen or heard of just about everything that can be done to their products.

Most engine modifications are concerned with improving the gas flow. To get maximum power from an engine it is essential to put into the combustion chamber the largest practicable amount of fuel.

This is often obtained by enlarging the inlet port, but when this is done a bigger-bore carburettor is required and manifolding must correspond. The standard carburettor is the best compromise the manufacturer could make to cope with both high speed on the road and traffic crawling.

I mentioned the choice of jets in the chapter on road racing. A bigger jet does not give more power; it simply makes the mixture richer. Apart from the guidance given by the appearance of plugs, if the power seems better with the throttle less than fully open then it suggests that the jet is too small; if the engine runs heavily it is probably too large.

In general, the higher the compression ratio the more power, and the sportsman will want the highest ratio at which the engine will run without distress. But compression ratio is dependent on the fuel to be used, the capacity and design of the engine, the composition of the head and the efficiency of the induction system.

Because exhaust systems may be dictated by considerations of design and appearance, larger-than-necessary pipes are sometimes fitted and performance may be aided by substituting pipes of smaller bore—particularly if racing camshafts are fitted.

The ideal exhaust-pipe length varies with speed and the maker has to decide where the exhaust is intended to function at its best. Megaphones used on racing machines give their best at the top of the power range and are less good at the bottom. By increasing their length greater torque can be obtained at the lower end of the range, but it will be lost at the top. Once again, one thing leads to another.

If the exhaust is modified a different-sized jet will be needed. For example if a racing machine with an open exhaust is fitted with a silencer for road running, the jet will need to be reduced or the running will be irregular.

It should be noted that in clubman's races it may be forbidden to use other than standard exhaust-systems and carburettors. Incidentally, for racing it may be advantageous to fit stronger clutch-springs than provided in a standard machine; they can be obtained from the maker.

When experimenting alter only one thing at a time. If timing and plugs, gear ratios and type of fuel are all altered at the same time one will learn nothing.

All changes should be entered in a log in the workshop. In it should also be noted the condition of parts on stripping and when new parts are fitted. And a record should be kept of each event entered with the carburettor settings, plugs used, gear ratios, compression ratio and other relevant data—and what happened in the event. Such a log will be found invaluable.

Personal tuning

Competitors give a lot of time and thought to tuning their machines. They should also consider the matter of keeping themselves in tune.

Different stars have different ideas, and, for that matter, different needs. Scrambler Jeff Smith believes in exercise to keep fit. He does twenty press-ups before breakfast and every week takes a 4-mile run to the top of a nearby hill. He also practises judo, which he says gives a motorcyclist valuable lessons in how to fall without getting hurt.

Other riders play football, lift weights or play squash. Others take little or no exercise apart from motorcycling. But, however fitness is achieved, fit one must be.

Do not take part in an exacting race if not feeling well; it is not fair to yourself or to other riders. And never eat a big meal or drink alcohol before an event.

14

Officials

EVERYONE taking part in motorcycle sport should know the duties and powers of the different officials. Remember that they are present to help, to make the meeting run smoothly. They do an essential job which may be tiring and uncomfortable and for which sometimes they may not receive even thanks. So their instructions should be obeyed without arguments.

You may be asked to act as a marshal yourself one day!

Stewards

The officials responsible for the supervision of a competition are the Stewards of the Meeting. There are three to five of them except in the case of a closed meeting, when there can be any number from one to five. The A.C.U. may nominate a majority of the stewards at any meeting and at a national meeting at least one of the stewards is A.C.U. nominated. A local centre which has granted a permit for a meeting may nominate one of the stewards, and if the meeting is a restricted one it invariably does so.

The stewards have no responsibility for the organization of the meeting, nor have they any executive duties in connection with it, but they are in supreme supervisory control over the carrying out of the programme in accordance with the regulations. It is their duty to ensure that the A.C.U.'s General Competition Rules are complied with, and to reprimand, fine or exclude from a competition or from the meeting anyone they find guilty of misbehaviour or unfair practice.

The stewards may, either on their own initiative or a request from the promoter or the Clerk of the Course, for urgent reasons of safety or other unavoidable necessity, postpone the start of a competition, modify the course, stop a competition prematurely or cancel the whole or part of a meeting, and no such decision can be questioned or challenged.

The stewards deal with protests arising out of the meeting. They may give summary judgment on any protest (subject to any right of appeal provided for in the rules) or may refer it for decision to the authority which granted the permit.

A steward is not allowed to undertake any other duty at the meeting, nor can he enter or ride in it.

In fact, no official is allowed to compete, for obvious reasons. Stewards are not paid, but receive hotel and travelling expenses.

Other officials

All other officials are nominated by the promoters, subject to the approval of the authority issuing the permit, and may be paid modestly for their services at a scale drawn up by the A.C.U.

The chief executive official at a competition is the Clerk of the Course, under whose orders come the following (as required by the type of competition):

> The Secretary of the Meeting
> Timekeepers
> Measurers
> Scrutineers
> Starters
> Judges
> Observers
> Handicappers

All executive officials may have assistants such as marshals and may be appointed to undertake several different duties, provided they have any necessary qualifications.

Let us look at the duties individually.

Clerk of the Course

The Clerk of the Course may also be the Secretary of the Meeting and may have various assistants. He is responsible to the stewards and to the promoter for the good management and conduct of a competition in accordance with the Supplementary Regulations and the official programme and for the direction of all officials necessary for that purpose. The Clerk of the Course controls the riders, and must prevent any rider or passenger excluded, suspended, disqualified, unqualified or otherwise ineligible from taking part in a competition. He must bar any rider, passenger or motorcycle he considers might be a source of danger.

If a rider commits an act or offence, for which the Supplementary Regulations provide that a penalty follows automatically, the Clerk of the Course must impose it. He can order the removal from the course of any person who refuses to obey an official's order. (He must, however, report his action immediately to the stewards.) He must report to the stewards any rider, passenger or other person he considers guilty of misbehaviour, unfair practice or failure to comply with rules and regulations and must pass on any protests promptly to the stewards.

He collects the reports of the timekeepers and other officials and prepares and publishes the provisional results of the meeting and any final amendments (or arranges for the Secretary of the Meeting to do so).

The Secretary of the Meeting

The Secretary of the Meeting is responsible particularly for the supply of all necessary documents and badges, and for dealing with official correspondence, and may act as the stewards' secretary.

He may undertake the duties of starter or judge or he may instruct a timekeeper or other officials to do so, except that in a competition where there is handicapping by time the starter must be a timekeeper. No protest may be made against the decision of a starter or judge.

Judges

Judges may be either starting judges, finishing judges or both. A starting judge's duty is to point out any false starts to the Clerk of the Course; the finishing judge's duty is to declare the order in which competitors crossed the finishing line. A judge may correct a mistake he has made if the stewards approve.

Timekeepers

The timekeepers report to the Clerk of the Course for their instructions and whether they are required to act as starters or judges, then record and report times required by the conditions of the competition.

Times are recorded to a fifth of a second, except when not more than two competitors are in competition together (for example, in special tests, hill climbs and speed trials), when the times may be recorded in either fifths or tenths of a second. It is an exacting job and the standards required are high.

Timekeepers are appointed annually by the A.C.U. In closed competitions the employment of an 'appointed' official is not necessary, but the A.C.U. will not take cognizance of any time-keeping dispute arising out of the event. In other competitions where exact timekeeping is concerned, the official to be employed must be approved beforehand by the authority granting the permit.

Every timekeeper must begin as a 'subsidiary', appointed by a local centre of the A.C.U. after taking practical tests involving timing the winner of a grass-track race, timing a short-distance competition by distant visual or audible signals and answering oral questions on A.C.U. rules and control of the sport.

After a year as a subsidiary he can apply to the A.C.U. for promotion to Grade B. To qualify he has to pass a written examination calling for the calculation of the speeds of winners in circuit races, answer oral questions and undergo practical tests similar to those for subsidiary timekeepers but with added tasks. These comprise timing, unaided, the passage on each lap of four to six riders in a race in which at least twelve are competing, and timing a series of grass-track or speedway races by keeping a lap record of every rider, timing the passage of the leader on each lap and noting the final times of the winner, second and third men, and compiling accurate records and reports.

After a year in Grade B a timekeeper can apply for further promotion—to Grade A—and after a year in Grade A he can apply for promotion to the ranks of national timekeepers. The tests for these appointments become progressively tougher.

International timekeepers are appointed by the F.I.M. on the recommendation of the A.C.U. Candidates for appointment must have been national timekeepers for at least two years and have to submit to further examinations.

Subsidiary timekeepers may officiate only at closed or restricted competitions held under the permit of the local centre which appointed them. Grade B timekeepers—there are a score of them —can officiate at these meetings and also in speedway, national trials and, under the supervision of a higher-grade timekeeper, at national scrambles. Grade A timekeepers—there are fewer of them—may officiate at these meetings, and, under the supervision of a higher-grade timekeeper, at national race-meetings.

The dozen national timekeepers can officiate at all competitions up to national level, including attempts at national records and, under the supervision of an international timekeeper, at international competitions.

The half-dozen international timekeepers are considered capable of timing anything!

Subsidiary timekeepers are unpaid. A and B grade men get three guineas a day and national and international timekeepers get five guineas a day; all appointed timekeepers also get hotel and travelling expenses, but they have to pay an annual fee on reappointment—10s. in the case of A and B grade men and £1 in the case of national and international clock-watchers.

Measurers
Measurers who check specifications of suspect machines are

appointed by the A.C.U. either annually or for a particular competition or, in the case of restricted or closed competitions, they may be appointed by a local centre.

Measurers pay a fee of 10s. each year on appointment or re-appointment, receive hotel and travelling expenses and may ask £1 for a meeting and an extra 10s. for each motorcycle measured.

Handicappers

Handicappers are appointed only for particular competitions and the timekeeper in charge of the meeting is eligible to undertake the handicapping. No protest can be made against the handicapper's deicsion. Handicappers may be paid fees and/or expenses by arrangement with the promoter.

H

15

Protests

ANY entrant or rider who feels aggrieved by any circumstance connected with a competition in which he is, or has been, taking part has the right to protest. This right should be used sparingly, reluctantly, for the 'barrack-room lawyer' is no more popular in sport than in the Services. But it is a good thing to know one's rights and so I will outline them here.

A protest has to be written out and accompanied by a fee—£1 if it is in connection with an international or national competition, 10s. in other cases. This fee will be returned only if the protest is held to be justified or upon a direction by the stewards of the meeting or the A.C.U.

Protests are heard by the stewards of the meeting after summoning the parties concerned. Their decisions are reached by a majority vote, the chairman having a casting vote when they are equally divided.

During a meeting protests should be handed to the Clerk of the Course or his representative; at other times they should be routed via the Secretary of the Meeting.

A protest about the validity of an entry or the eligibility of a ride has to be lodged before the start of a competition—24 hours before in national competitions—except when conditions make this impossible. Then it must be made with the minimum of delay and, at the latest, within half an hour of the end of the competition.

A protest against a decision by a measurer or scrutineer must be lodged immediately.

A protest about any mistake or irregularity which may have occurred during a race must be made within 10 minutes of the finish. Protests lodged after this time will not be considered unless the stewards are satisfied that there was no unnecessary delay and give their permission.

A protest concerning the results of a competition or other matters must be lodged within five days of publication of the detailed results.

An award gained by an entrant or rider against whom a protest has been lodged is withheld until the protest has been ruled on and any appeal has been decided or the time for an appeal has passed.

I will deal with the subject of appeals later.

Penalties

Any form of sport has to have machinery to deal with breaches of the rules or misbehaviour. In the case of motorcycle sport the stewards of a meeting can, as I said in the last chapter, reprimand, fine or exclude from a competition or from the meeting any rider they find guilty of misbehaviour or unfair practice. They can also report such a person to the A.C.U. for further disciplinary action.

Other disciplinary matters, complaints and disputes are adjudicated upon by special courts. These are set up by the local centre in cases relating to local clubs and by the A.C.U. in cases relating to bigger matters and to the sport generally. (In a territory administered by a national club the club sets up its own court.)

Among the cases courts may have to hear are breaches of the rules, attempted bribery of officials, attempts to compete by an ineligible person or the entry of an ineligible machine, and acts prejudicial to the sport generally.

Penalties may be a reprimand, a fine, exclusion, suspension or disqualification. (For participating in an unauthorized competition the penalties are always disqualification or suspension.)

A *reprimand* needs no explanation.

Fines (which go into the A.C.U. Benevolent Fund) have to be paid within ten days of their being ordered; a delay in making payment will entail suspension until the fine is paid.

Exclusion means the prohibition from taking part in a particular capacity or in any capacity in a certain competition or meeting.

Suspension means prohibition for a time or indefinite period of a person—or machine or make or accessory—from motorcycle competitions within certain territories, according to whether the suspension is international, national or local.

Local suspension, which may be pronounced by the A.C.U., a local centre or national club, means the loss of the right to take part in any closed or restricted competition within the territory of the local centre or national club.

National suspension may be pronounced by the same bodies, but in the case of a local centre or national club it has to be confirmed by the A.C.U. and if they refuse it has the effect only of local suspension.

International suspension, which can be pronounced only by the A.C.U. and has to be confirmed by the F.I.M., means the loss of the right to take part in any competition in any country where the F.I.M.'s authority is recognized. It also bars the offender from taking part in motor, motorboat and flying competitions.

Suspension renders void any entry already made for a competition.

Disqualification means the loss for all time of the right to take part in any motorcycle, motor, motorboat or flying competition in any country. It can be pronounced only by the A.C.U. and has to be confirmed by the F.I.M., who are also the only body which can restore the lost rights.

Any entrant, driver or passenger who is excluded, suspended or disqualified in a competition forfeits all right to an award in that competition.

The Courts

A court consists of three to five persons with no direct interest in the case. The rules of the Auto-Cycle Union have legal authority, and decisions of the Union's courts will be upheld by courts of law provided such decisions are within the scope of the rules and that elementary principles of justice have been observed. In fact, the Union's courts follow the pattern of courts of law.

Adequate notice of a hearing must be given to all parties concerned by registered post. All parties concerned are entitled to call witnesses, and they and their witnesses must be given an opportunity of being heard. If, however, the parties concerned have declared in writing that they do not intend to appear in person before the court then the court may deal with the matter without them.

In a prosecution, the nature of the charge against the defendant has to be made clear, specifying the rule or rules he is charged with having broken and, where the rule is in general terms, giving particulars of the actual offence.

The court is forbidden to discuss the case before the actual hearing. All parties directly concerned are allowed to be present throughout the proceedings, except when the court confers to reach a decision. Witnesses may be excluded before giving their evidence and may be required to remain in court after giving it.

The court is not empowered to take evidence on oath except when sitting as a court of arbitration.

The proceedings are private; members of the public, the Press and other officials of the A.C.U. are not entitled to be present, though the court may give permission for visitors to attend.

The parties directly concerned may be represented by solicitor or counsel or by any other person permitted to do so by leave of the court, provided reasonable notice has been given to the court and other parties directly concerned. A party represented should not address the court himself unless called upon.

On the hearing of appeals the court must call for the record of the previous proceedings and determine whether the principles of procedure laid down in the rules have been followed.

Where it has imposed a fine or sentence of exclusion, suspension or disqualification, the court may make an order as to costs as it deems fit, but such an order made by the stewards of a meeting or a local centre is subject to confirmation by the A.C.U.

Protest or appeal fees are not normally refunded by the court except where it is considered that the protest or appeal has advanced the interest of the sport. All courts must cause 'a suitable and sufficient record' of proceedings to be kept.

Appeals

Any person affected by a decision of the stewards of a meeting has a right of appeal to the authority that granted the permit for the meeting or to a higher authority.

In the case of meetings promoted by a local centre or national club the appeal may be made instead to the A.C.U., and in the case of meetings promoted by the A.C.U. and international meetings in A.C.U. territory an appeal may be made instead to the stewards of the R.A.C.

Notices of appeal, like protests, have to be in writing and accompanied by the appeal fee. Appeals are comparatively expensive: £5 for an appeal to a local centre, £10 to the A.C.U. and £10 10s. to the R.A.C. They should be addressed to the secretary of the appropriate authority.

The time limit for an appeal is thirty days in the case of appeals arising out of an international meeting, ten days in others, the time being from the notification of the decision appealed against.

It should be noted that no one at all has the power to authorize the re-running of a competition, once it is over.

Competitor's Encyclopaedia

(based on A.C.U. definitions)

A.C.U.—Auto-Cycle Union, a branch of the Royal Automobile Club, consisting of national clubs (for example, Australia), non-territorial clubs and clubs forming local centres. It is responsible to the F.I.M. for the administration of motorcycle sport throughout the British Commonwealth except for Canada and Northern Ireland.

Appeal—A formal demand to a higher tribunal for relief from the decision of a lower one.

Classic—A title which may be given by the A.C.U. to certain meetings of traditional importance to be given priority in the annual calendar.

Clerk of the Course—the chief executive official at a meeting.

Clubs—A national club is a club affiliated to the A.C.U. and controlling the sport in Scotland or a British Commonwealth country, colony or dependency overseas. A non-territorial club is a club having at least 100 members which is affiliated directly to the A.C.U. and not through a local centre. There are also local clubs.

Competition—Any trial, race, record attempt or sporting occasion (other than a gymkhana or social event) in which one or more motorcyclists compete, either against each other or the clock, or attempt to fulfil certain conditions laid down in advance. Competitions may be International, Extra-national, Restricted or Closed. An International competition is one which is open to riders of more than one nation, except that a competition open only to riders of the British Commonwealth and Ireland is called Extra-national. A National competition is one open to riders holding appropriate licences issued by the A.C.U. or a national club. A Regional Restricted competition is one when the qualification is concerned with residence or membership of clubs in an area greater than one centre. A Centre Restricted competition is open only to members of clubs in the local centre concerned. A Closed competition is open only to members of one club.

Course—The route to be followed in a competition.

C.S.I.—Commission Sportive Internationale, the international sporting commission of the F.I.M.

Cylinder volume—The volume swept in a cylinder or cylinders by the upward or downward movement of the piston or pistons, expressed in cubic centimetres.

Disqualification—The loss for all time of any right to take part in any way in any competition.

Driver—The A.C.U.'s word for a person of sixteen or over nominated to ride a motorcycle in a competition.

Exclusion—Prohibition of a person or body of persons from taking a particular part or any part in a certain competition, or the prohibition of a certain motorcycle, make of motorcycle or accessory from being used.

F.I.M.—Federation Internationale Motocycliste. The international motorcycle federation, top authority of the sport.

F.M.N.—Federation Motocycliste Nationale, a national motorcycling organization recognized by the F.I.M. as the governing body of the sport in its own territory (for example, the A.C.U.).

Grand Prix—A title which may be given once a year by the A.C.U. to one meeting of each of the following types: 1, a race, whether road, track, speedway, grass or hill climb; 2, motocross; 3, a trial; 4, a rally; 5, motorcycle football.

Grass-track race—A race on a continuous grass circuit.

Handicap—A method laid down in the Supplementary Regulations of a competition, having as its purpose the equalizing of the chances of the competitors as far as possible. Handicaps may be published or sealed; that is, not published to the competitors until a time fixed by the Supplementary Regulations.

Heat—One of a series of races, the whole of which constitutes a particular competition.

Hill climb—A race from point to point, including the climbing of a steep gradient, between two or more competitors at a time or against time.

Kilometres—A kilometre is 0·6213720 mile, while a mile equals 1·6093440 kilometres.

Local centre—Clubs (other than non-territorial clubs) in the same A.C.U. area together make up a local centre.

Meeting—An assembly of riders and officials at which one or more competitions, other than an individual attempt on a record, are held. A meeting is not ended until after the publication of results.

Moto-cross—A cross-country race presenting irregularities of surface or terrains.

Motorcycle football—A team competition in which the riders of motorcycles manoeuvre a ball.

Motorcycles—Mechanically propelled vehicles with fewer than four wheels, which are divided into the following categories: solo motorcycles and solo scooters which are one-track vehicles with two road wheels, and sidecar outfits and cyclecars which are three-wheelers. Each category is divided into classes with a minimum and maximum cylinder volume, each class being described by its maximum cylinder volume.

Nationality—The nationality of a rider, in the eyes of the A.C.U., is that of the national motorcycle federation which last issued him a licence.

Officials—Are supervisory, administrative or executive. Supervisory officials are the stewards of a meeting. Executive and administrative officials are the Clerk of the Course, Secretary of the Meeting, Starter, Judge, technical officials and marshals who carry out the detailed organization of a competition.

Outside assistance—An act by anyone other than the rider, passenger (if carried) or an official in the course of his duty, which involves contact with the vehicle.

Passengers—Must be sixteen or over and weigh, kitted out, not less than 132 pounds.

Permit—The documentary authority to organize and hold one or more competitions, granted by the F.I.M. in the case of international events and the A.C.U. or local centres in others.

Promoter—Any person or body proposing to hold or organize a meeting.

Protest—A formal statement of objection to an alleged irregularity on the part of a person concerned in a competition.

R.A.C.—Royal Automobile Club, governing body of British motor sport, from which control of motorcycling events is delegated to the A.C.U.

Race—A competition in which speed determines the result.

Rally—A *competitive* rally is a trial taking place over various routes converging on a rallying point fixed in advance, and in which the average speed is limited. A *social* rally is an event organized with the primary object of assembling tourists at a point fixed in advance.

Records—Are best results obtained under prescribed conditions. For a *world's record* these are prescribed by the F.I.M.; for a *national record* by the A.C.U.

Road race—A race on a roadway or other prepared surface having the characteristics of an ordinary highway, and continuous in circuit.

Sand race—A race on the seashore, either on a continuous circuit or from point to point.

Scramble—See Moto-cross.

Speed trial—A race from point to point on a good surface on level ground and over a measured distance between two or more competitors at a time or against time.

Speedway—An enclosed area comprising a loose-surfaced track, continuous in circuit, with one or more stands for the public.

Starts—*Flying starts* are made when speed up to the starting line is not restricted; *rolling starts* when speed up to the starting line is restricted; *standing starts* when motorcycles are stationary and engines dead until the order to start is given; *clutch starts* when motorcycles are stationary but engines are running until the order to start is given. When competitors start singly it is an *individual start*; when all are started together it is a *mass start*.

Supplementary Regulations—Regulations complementary to the General Competition Rules and Standing Regulations of the A.C.U. and relating to the details of a competition, which are drawn up by the promoter of a competition and approved.

Suspension—The prohibition of a person or body of persons from taking part in certain competitions, or the prohibition of a certain motorcycle or make of motorcycle or accessory from being used.

Track—A permanent or temporary course utilized for competitions. A permanent course is laid out for racing and generally has pits and a stand for the accommodation of the public. It is licensed by the A.C.U. Unlicensed courses may have certificates as temporary courses.

Track race—A race other than a road race on a closed circuit, the surface of which is hard and continuous. It may or may not be banked on bends.

Trial—A competition in which a number of riders take part, endeavouring to fulfil prescribed conditions.

APPENDIX II

Useful Addresses

Auto-Cycle Union (Secretary, K. E. Shierson), 31 Belgrave Square, London, S.W.1. 01–235 7636.

F.I.M., 7 Rue Carteret, Geneva, Switzerland.

National clubs

Australia: Auto-Cycle Council of Australia, Savoy Buildings, Elgin Street, Maitland, New South Wales.

British Guiana: British Guiana Motor Racing Club, 9 Commerce Street, Georgetown.

Ceylon: Ceylon M.C.C., P.O. Box 1111, Mungoor Building, Colombo 11.

East Africa: A.A. of East Africa, P.O. Box 87, Nairobi, Kenya.

Malaya: Automobile Association of Malaya, P.O. Box 150, Penang.

Malta: Malta Automobile and Cycle Racing Association, 35 Old Bakery Street, Valetta.

New Zealand: New Zealand A.C.U., P.O. Box 648, Hamilton.

Rhodesia: Rhodesia Motor Sports Association, P.O. Box 1459, Bulawayo.

Scotland: Scottish A.C.U. (T. Arnott Moffat), 23 Torpichen Street, Bathgate. West Lothian. Bathgate 2637.

Singapore: Singapore M.C., P.O. Box 20, Newtown Post Office.

Zambia: Ndola M.S.C., Box 1152, Ndola.

English-speaking F.I.M. countries

Canada: Canadian Motorcycle Association, Box 100, Islington, Ontario.

Ireland: Motorcycle Union of Ireland, 11 Glen Crescent, Whiteabbey, Newtownabbey, N. Ireland.

South Africa: A.A. of South Africa, De Villiers Street, P.O. Box 596, Johannesburg.

Important British clubs

Army Motorcycling Association (Lt.-Col. J. G. C. Low): Army Mechanical Transport School, Bordon, Hampshire.

Bantam Racing Club (T. Reading): 49 Barnham Road, Greenford, Middlesex.

British Drag Racing and Hot Rod Association (Mrs. A. Bennett): 48 Whitehorse Lane, South Norwood, London, S.E.25.

British Motorcycle Racing Club (J. H. Swift): P.O. Box 75, 33a London Road, Kingston-on-Thames, Surrey.

British Two Stroke Club (R. Pratley): 62 Flamstead Road, Strelley, Notts.

Civil Service Motoring Association Ltd. (S. L. J. Cook): 4 Norris Street, Haymarket, London, S.W.1.

Honda Owners Club of Great Britain (A. E. J. Eldridge): 26 Sherwood Road, Barkingside, Ilford, Essex.

International Motorcyclists Tour Club, Rally Section (B. J. Arthur): 14 Sheffield Terrace, London, W.8.

Motorcycling Club Ltd. (R. L. Archer): 70 Stoneleigh Road, Clayhall, Ilford, Essex.

Motorcycling Club of Wales (G. Gosling): 52 East Road, Tylorstown, Ferndale, Glamorganshire.

National Sprint Association (J. T. Terry): 96 Carlton Avenue West, North Wembley, Middlesex.

Racing 50 M.C.C. (A. W. Laid): 13 Olma Road, Dunstable, Beds.

Triumph Owners Motorcycle Club (A. Walker): 3 Conway, Constitution Hill, Benfleet, Essex.

Vintage M.C.C. (Eric E. Thompson): 28 Glover Road, Pinner, Middlesex.